Piecework

Ethnographies of Place

Amy Shimshon-Santo

For information contact:
Unsolicited Press
Portland, Oregon
www.unsolicitedpress.com
orders@unsolicitedpress.com
619-354-8005

Cover Design: Sammy Savos
Editor: S.R. Stewart
ISBN: 978-1-963115-29-1

Also by Amy Shimshon-Santo

Poetry

Random Experiments in Bioluminescence

Catastrophic Molting

Even the Milky Way is Undocumented

Endless Bowls of Sky

Anthologies

Et Al.: New Voices in Arts Management with Genevieve Kaplan

Corpos, Gêneros, e Autoria Feminina with Ana Rita Santiago & Tatiana Pequeno

Arts = Education

"Space is another world. Place is where you want to place them."

—Reva Santo (4 years old)

"If you say 'it's a space' then it is *your* space. 'That's *my* space.' 'That's *your* space.' If they say 'it's a place' then it is not yours. It is everybody's."

—Avila Santo (6 years old)

"Place is established not just through practice but through naming, storytelling, and genealogies — through the culturing of people's encounter with each other and the world."

—Dr. Damon Salesa (51 years old)

"Silent friends of many distances, feel
how your breath enlarges all of space.
Let your presence ring out like a bell into the night."

—Rainer Maria Rilke (Deceased)

CONTENTS

I'm In a Relationship with an Essay

CLASSROOMS

Teachers Were Children Too   13

Creative Justice: Arts Education for the City   16

Connecting the Dots   42

Arts Education for the Next Generation of Culture Makers   61

COMMUNITIES

"Do Our Lives Matter?": music, poetry, and Freedom School   76

Born in Los Angeles on Los Angeles Street   97

How to Become Erasure Proof   105

MIGRATIONS

My Grandma Was a Radical   147

פ   180

Facing East   185

CONVERSATIONS

Writing Can be a Freedom Vessel   195

Bodies, Genders, and Authoring the Feminine   201

Pep Talk for Culture Makers   206

Acknowledgments   211

Notes   214

Works Cited   220

Piecework

Ethnographies of Place

I'm In a Relationship with an Essay

My daughter maintains an archive of strange things people say. One afternoon she scrolled through her smartphone to cite me back to myself. "Here it is," she said grinning. "I'm in a relationship with an essay." I must have blurted that out one day between the desk and the kitchen, while shifting from writing to mothering-mode. The essays in this book were written at home and my children were often my witnesses. As an artist, mother, and teacher, writing essays challenged me to pay attention to what was going on within and around us. This collection honors the life force of numerous children and adults in schools, communities, and homes. *Piecework* is a compilation of essays that reflect on collective action. They are ethnographies and auto-ethnographies of place with some poems sprinkled in. I hope that this book inspires activists, teachers, and families to tell their own stories and share them with their communities.

I became a mother in my twenties and ended up raising two fabulous human beings as a single parent. My "career" snaked through a life in dance, capoeira, urban planning, teaching, teaching teachers, community arts, launching start ups, growing programs, and writing. My love of teaching connected me with schools, community centers, and research universities where I worked with people across the life cycle: from kindergartners to doctoral candidates, and from artists to nonprofit leaders.

Writing has been important to having a good life. I journaled, wrote poems, and drafted one slow-growth ethnographic essay at a time while raising children as a head of household. Eventually, my poems and essays became published and I could share them with more than close friends.

Telling our stories and expanding the archive is an important part of social justice work. When I began teaching, I could not find much written about arts education or community arts practice from the perspectives of multi-diasporic families and communities like mine. I always felt a divide between home and the university and labored to mend the gap. My approach to research became: make yourself useful and create knowledge. Share what you learn for multiple publics.

There are many ways to write. Coming from a background in dance, I consider movement and music to be languages. My father used to say, "writing is thinking." He wrote from outlines: 1, 2, 3. A, B, C. A linear approach felt impossible to me. Free verse and performance came more naturally. I did not learn how to write an essay until I went to college. The basic form of an introduction, conclusion, and three body paragraphs looked like two arrows pointing inward, and three rectangular idea cartridges. However, I slowly adapted to working with essay structures and became familiar with their architecture.

The etymology of the word essay means to weigh, ascertain, or try. Essays are good for asking questions, and I like that. They are also well suited for sharing an inquiry process with readers.

Writing essays helped me think for myself. I didn't always feel empowered to speak in my own voice about what I intimately knew. I found it odd to not be able to mention myself as a knower in social science essays, or to refer to an idea without being able to cite it from a previously published text. Without an inclusive bibliography, how would I write about the worlds of knowledge around me?

As far as I know, I don't come from writers. The people I knew were dancing, making music, painting, singing, creating sculpture, and telling stories. They were organizing for social and political change to defend immigrants and working people. Writing ethnography and autoethnography, participant observation and interviews, became ways for me to write about the unpublished dynamics of home, community, and place that surrounded me. I could write about women's and children's lives, and the classrooms and community spaces I was involved with. While I've written white papers and policy statements that set precedents for action, ethnography reveals how things actually play out on the ground.

Motherhood, teaching, and community work are vital, yet too often undervalued. My essays reflected on what I witnessed listening to children and adults, and what I learned through culture and art as valuable knowledge. Writing auto-ethnography provided the reflexivity I needed to become a protagonist in my own life. At the same time, my children grew into adults who write music, lyrics, screenplays, multimedia art works, essays, and poems. My former students author dances, prose, poetry and lead creative spaces, companies, classrooms, and policy debates.

How does a single mother wrangle time to write? When my son and daughter entered pre-school, I returned to school too. We spent evenings studying around the kitchen table with snacks. I resorted to reading homework aloud in a soft tone to the kids as good night stories that helped them fall asleep. By kindergarten, my youngest could read the Italian political philosopher Antonin Gramsci aloud, and my eldest had contributed his views on space and place in an email conversation with the geographer Edward Soja. As my kids grew, I taught just above their grade levels to prepare myself for what was coming next.

We made our home into a makeshift multimedia art studio. An unfurnished living room can be an open space for choreography, and a kitchen table is a good place for poetry workshops. We wrote, read, made music, danced, played capoeira, and experimented with every analogue and digital technology we could get our hands on.

Midlife is a time of reflection. The essays I wrote are a record of relationships with communities. I was never offered a job that required me to "publish or perish," but I believed that writing was important to do. These essays honor the miraculous ways that everyday people author their own lives, learning, and places.

CLASSROOMS

The book is clustered into three themes. The classrooms section begins with a playful glimpse into my early identity formation in elementary school in "Teachers Were Children Too," and gathers three essays set in classrooms as spaces for learning. The essays include: "Creative Justice: Arts Education for the City," "Connecting the Dots," and "Arts Education for the Next Generation of Culture Makers."

"Creative Justice: Arts Education for the City," is a multi-classroom ethnography. Like many teaching artists, I guided hundreds of arts residencies. In the #ElaraMoves Project, I worked with students and four classroom teachers in technology, design, writing, and visual art. Together, we studied Safe Routes to School (SRTS) in East Los Angeles. SRTS aims to make sure that children and youth can arrive and return home safely to school each day. That is not the case for many children and youth. In #ElaraMoves, students used the arts and design to perform original social research about transportation and mobility in their neighborhood. They also created work that I designed into a community publication called #ElaraMoves. When we completed the project, we welcomed their book into their school library with a participatory book launch. Afterward, I wrote an essay about the process to reflect on what I learned along the way. This essay became useful for other educators and community activists when designing their own methodologies and curricula.

I wrote "Connecting the Dots" while directing a teaching artist preparation program that aimed to prepare artists to teach and welcome first generation teens into college. I thought of it as an in-reach/outreach program. After working as a teaching artist for 19 years, I was recruited to help prepare teaching artists and create collaborations with urban school districts in Los Angeles. Most of the writing I had to produce around that time was curriculum or reports, so I welcomed the chance to reflect on local work in the good company of community artists and popular education activists throughout the Americas.

30 years into tinkering with arts education pedagogy, I was invited to join a team of documentarians to create an arts education documentary for public television. We designed the film project but were forced to adapt our approach when schools shuttered during the pandemic. The project was completed under unimaginable social conditions and earned an Emmy Award nomination. I wrote "Arts Education for the Next Generation of Culture Makers" as a companion piece to the documentary so readers could imagine being inside the schools we had scouted and observed before school closures.

COMMUNITIES

The second section of the book shares essays about projects completed with community centers or museums. "Do Our Lives Matter?" tells the story of co-teaching with my son, Avila Santo, for the Community Coalition (COCO) in South Los Angeles. In the COCO Art Lab project, we offered arts education to youth while focusing on critical thinking and political leadership development. The youth organizing in this essay confronted a series of high-profile racist murders. Seventeen-year-old Trayvon Martin had been killed by the vigilante George Zimmerman shortly before the residency began, and Philando Castile was murdered by police officer Jeronimo Yanez during the residency. The title for this essay came from a conversation facilitated with youth about the senseless murders of Black and Brown children. The youth activists brainstormed ways of amplifying their lives and voices through music and poetry that culminated in blog publications, a poster series to help get out the vote, and a public performance with the grammy-award winning artist Bilal Oliver.

I wrote "Born in Los Angeles on Los Angeles Street" to honor the life of Manuela C. Garcia. Janice Ngan had invited me to write a poem about an artifact — a wax cylinder with Garcia's voice — for the Autry Museum archive. By that time, I had shifted my creative practice from dance to poetry, but I could not write a poem without knowing about Garcia on her own terms. Up until that point, she had been studied as an "informant" to Charles Lummis but had yet to be written about as a culture bearer in her own right. When I asked the museum to see her personal journal, her handwriting unleashed an expansive multinational project studying her life from the perspectives of poetry, sound, mariachi music, Chicano studies, and transnational music publishing in the Americas.

The collection finishes with "How to Become Erasure Proof" — a geo-humanities essay that reveals significant, multi-centered, intergenerational cultural ecologies of place keeping in Los Angeles. I welcomed the chance to gather friends, family, and students to reflect about sustaining grassroots creative spaces. Before I became a mother, I co-founded the Brasil Brasil Cultural Center in Los Angeles. I raised my children in a space where generations of capoeiristas, poets, dancers, and musicians grew into their powers as creators, culture bearers, and teachers. "Erasure Proof" centers a community conversation on place with BIPOC cultural catalysts from Leimert Park, Boyle Heights, and Little Tokyo in Los Angeles. For me, this essay marked an important circle of life. I hope that readers enjoy the wisdom participants conveyed about the stewardship of land, story, archives, and leadership.

MIGRATIONS

The third section of the book points to family, diasporas, and heritage. I came into higher education from community work creating art and organizing, and my worldview was shaped by those formative experiences. I wanted study and research to expand possibilities for women, children, and families in immigrant and aggrieved communities. After many years advocating for systemic and policy changes, I wanted the freedom to speak in my own voice without gatekeepers, boards of directors, or politicians weighing in on what I could say. This inspired me to return to graduate school later in life to study creative writing. While my daughter entered undergraduate studies in film and my son completed a BA in music, I dug into writing essays and poems.

I had a visceral reaction to touching the pages of Jonathan Safran Foer's *Tree of Codes*, a book of erasures made from Bruno Schulz' *Street of Crocodiles*. My body recognized that I came from a people who had not written or been written about in English. I wanted to take this responsibility seriously and find something from my own lineage that I could read. Biking home from school in the dark, it occurred to me that I might be able to find my paternal grandmother's testimony before the House Un-American Activities Committee (HUAC). Sure enough, I tracked it down online along with numerous FBI documents recovered through the Freedom of Information Act. These artifacts revealed stories about Reva Mucha's life and social movements of the 1950s. I even unearthed a letter in the W.E.B. Dubois archive addressed to her. This inquiry process became the essay "My Grandma Was a Radical."

To intentionally balance my mother and father's lineages, I have included poems inspired from my maternal legacy. She was born a Jew in British Mandate Palestine. My grandparents and great grandparents lived there during the Ottoman Empire. My maternal history exists in different contexts and languages. Grappling with this is part of my homework for the future.

I wrote "Facing East" to weave a coherent story across six generations that embraced complexity and multiplicity. This story became a vessel that could hold Jewishness, Blackness, and multiple diasporic connections. The meaning of artworks can continue to change over time in miraculous and unexpected ways. This essay speaks to the cultural connectivity and expansiveness of my own family.

For those who like behind-the-scenes accounts, I included excerpts from translocal interviews with colleagues in Brazil and Nigeria. The book ends with a word about community and intergenerational work.

As an artist, mother, and teacher, writing essays challenged me to reflect on our everyday acts of personal and social change. One essay at a time, writing helped me find meaning in deep and enduring connections to family, community, and place.

CLASSROOMS

Grade 3, Mr. Washington's classroom, Will Roger's Elementary School.

Teachers Were Children Too

I love fresh kinesthetic experiences. Swing and throw. Hit and catch. Cheer our movements on. When I was a kid, girls did not get to do that in school.

In kindergarten, my sister and I walked to the principal's office to ask for permission to wear pants. Pants are superior attire for a fabulous recess. Sitting on a bench to keep your dress tidy is grand life larceny. Handball is better in pants. So are kickball, hopscotch, tetherball, and tops. Loop the cord on your middle finger and a hard wooden object with a nail at the tip would be ready for battle.

Playgrounds and classrooms are sites for small revolutions as we learn how to be and what is possible. In third grade, Black is beautiful. Mom walks precincts to get out the vote. I bet a dime on an election and lose my hard-won savings but earn a lesson in politics. The best does not always win. We still must know the difference between crooked and trustworthy and do the right thing.

During earthquake drills we crouched beneath tables, heads between our knees. But no one prepared me to defend my desire to play. By the time Title IX passed, I'd picked the lock to the classroom and pleaded to switch schools. There were no sports in alternative school, but I would learn the necessary survival skills of muralism, adopting mice, embroidery, contact improvisation, theater, and how to make a bag from an old pair of pants.

My father's dad visited California. He brought a basketball for my brother, and a useless plastic Barbie with dyslexic feet for me. I felt crushed, furious, claustrophobic, heartbroken, and planning my escape. Thankfully, my Pop let me trade it for a football. Street ball with my brothers was open hydrant fun in the heat wave of kid-dom. As quarterback, I could throw an object far into space and we could score.

By age six, kids had dubbed me *TomBoy Women's Libber.* Call me what you will. I am a somatic. Movement is sublime, and I am one of those kinds of persons.

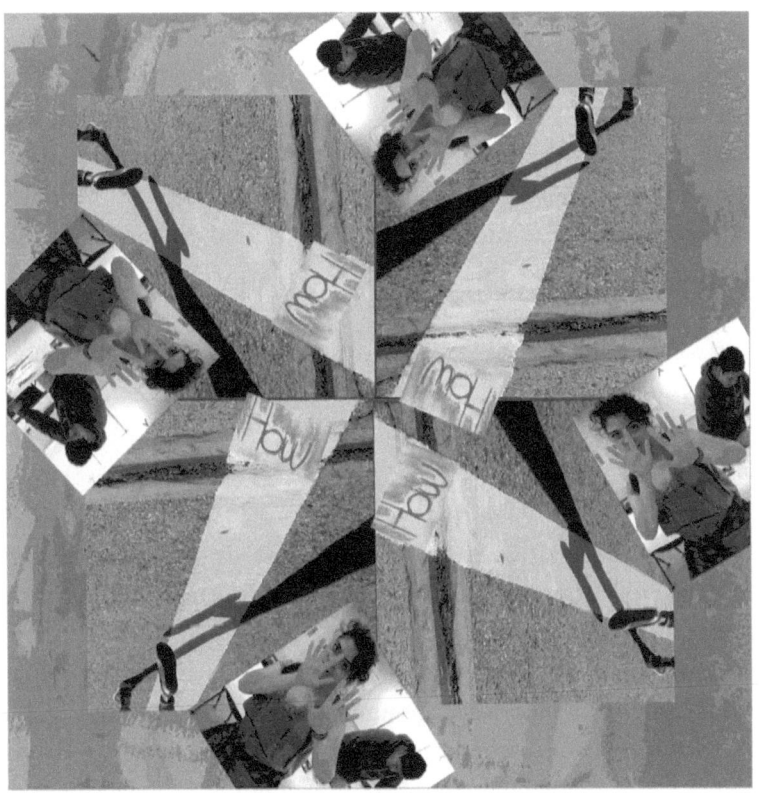

Safe Routes to School Project. Collage: Author.

Creative Justice: Arts Education for the City

"Transportation is a big factor in our lives — especially people like me who ride the bus." Angel's voice echoed against the library walls. Sunlight streamed in through the windows illuminating rows of seats jammed with spectators at the culmination of our project, which began in January. It was May and graduation was around the corner. "I realize that you want to make things better for — not yourself — but for the people" (Public Testimony 2015b). The crowd applauded, shouting affirmations. Angel had accomplished more than learning about transportation or the arts; he'd made connections, formed opinions, and inspired others with his voice.

This essay is geared for arts educators and urban planners who are interested in socially engaged research with youth. Youth are a powerhouse for creative cities. However, the discourse on creativity and urban development rarely prioritizes the perspectives of young people of color in decision-making about urban spaces. Here I discuss the #Elara Moves project (EM) — a school-wide art integration and participatory research process about mobility in East Los Angeles. I led EM with a team of teachers and students from the East Los Angeles Renaissance Academy (ELARA), facilitating, analyzing, and circulating youth knowledge about Safe Routes to School (SRTS) in the community. Studying the city through the arts allowed teenagers to amplify local knowledge, practice leadership, and envision alternative futures. Along the way, students cultivated agency as the heroes and heroines of their own stories, and learned how to intervene in urban systems that impact their daily lives.

Media Messaging Activity. Photos: Author.

RESEARCH PROCESS

We began the project with participatory planning between me and an interdisciplinary team of teachers: Hector Verduzco (New Media), Michael Rocha (Journalism), John Lee (Drawing), and Martin Buchman (Administrative Coordinator). We decided on the mobility focus, branded the project #ELARA Moves in order to archive and circulate knowledge on social media, and agreed to make a process book as a learning outcome. Instruction took place from January through May 2015, with 82 ninth and twelfth graders.

Our key research question was "How do ELARA students get around?" Three core ideas about knowledge guided how I facilitated our research: 1. The arts are a powerful tool for creative inquiry about people and places. 2. Youth perspectives are important for understanding local conditions and making informed city-planning decisions. 3. Engaging teens in community-based inquiry inspires youth development. Students studied mobility through the four pillars of SRTS: safety, health, community, and choice.

The EM research process is akin to both participatory action research (PAR) and arts- based research (Fals Borda 2013; McIntyre 2000; Rolling 2013b; Barone and Eisner 2012). For Fals Borda, PAR prioritizes the expertise of everyday people, and grasps the connections between analytical and intuitive knowledge, or *sentipensando* (thinking-feeling). McIntyre distinguishes PAR as a "collective commitment to investigate an issue or problem . . . a desire to engage in self and collective reflection; . . . action that leads to a useful solution which benefits the people involved" (2000, 15). Arts Based Research emphasizes "the forms of thinking and . . . representation that the arts provide" (Barone and Eisner 2012, xi). It provides "a flexible architecture for representing the world . . . grounded in the local site of inquiry (Rolling 2013b, 49).

Arts integration combines more than one content area for learning. In EM, SRTS was our thematic trellis for teaching urban studies and the arts. Drawing on years of community-based arts-making, I wove information about SRTS into art-making activities in a range of classes. Journalism students wrote stories about notable trips to and from school, interviewed community members, and practiced co-creation through performance. Fine art students created photographs, drawings, paintings, and prints about modes of transportation, streets, and the built environment. They studied visual composition and design while illustrating ideas from the journalism students' writing, and inventing typefaces for the EM publication. The new media students mapped and analyzed their transportation routes with digital technology and used image capture to report on danger getting to and from school, including poor illumination and collision-prone street corners. We analyzed student mobility survey data using Google Form analytics and critical discussions with students, and videoed student findings to share on YouTube.

Mobility conveys freedom of movement and is critical to the livability and sustainability of households, neighborhoods, cities, and regions. We sought mobility to get around the city in safe, affordable, and healthy ways that connect residents to affordable housing, public parks, quality schools, healthy food, work, and career options.

I focused EM participatory research on SRTS because of its immediate relevance to youth. SRTS is a national mobility movement that aims to increase safety and access to active transportation (such as biking, walking, and skateboarding), encourage healthy lifestyles that improve public health, decrease carbon emissions to improve air quality, and foster neighborhood connections among students, families, school officials, and community leaders. SRTS expands mobility choices for young people, especially children who are marginalized in underserved areas. EM helped ELARA students inform themselves about mobility options, develop their own opinions about SRTS, and advocate for positive changes in the community.

EM circulated youth knowledge about SRTS through exhibitions, public speaking, blogging, social media, and a publication. I created a process blog (i.e., a simple website) to amplify student learning and shared field notes to display in class. Students enjoyed being digital influencers and knowing they reached people locally and nationally. We used social media to amplify youth voices, disrupt geographic isolation, and help students envision online professional identities. They studied how to circulate information to broader audiences on Twitter and Instagram and witnessed how their ideas spread through "retweets" and "likes."

Line studies with the built environment. Photos: Author.

CONCEPTUAL FRAMEWORK

Youth in the Creative City

Los Angeles is home to over ten million residents, 23% of whom are under the age of eighteen. As an urban planner, I care about how children shape and are marked by where they live and learn. As an artist, I know that residents of all ages and cultures can shape creative cities to be inclusive and sustainable. Cities are contested spaces shaped by histories of power and negotiation, inclusion and exclusion, destruction, and renewal. Actively seeking to improve living and learning conditions for youth is critical to the cultural vitality of cities.

The role of creativity in enhancing urban life, creating a sense of place, and spurring economic activity has been widely studied (Markusen and Gadwa 2010; Florida 2005; Jackson 2014). However, less attention has been paid to roles for marginalized youth as future leaders of creative cities. James Haywood Rolling Jr. theorizes creativity as a powerful social force. He explains that "creativity originates as a social behavior, not an individual one. We think of *his* creativity or *her* creativity, but rarely do we think of *our* creativity" (Rolling 2013a, 6). Sarah Bainter Cunningham sees arts education of children as critical for urban spaces. She writes,

> Arts educators may be the crucial lynchpin to providing residents with the ability to meet their needs and articulate their own voice in shaping the city. Art and design literacies enable...children to make claims on what the city could be (Bainter Cunningham 2013, 6).

As an artist and urbanist, I enjoy learning what kids think, what they have seen and overcome, and what they find funny, frightening, or inspiring about their communities. I facilitate mutual respect for student knowledge, and guide students through activities where they can take risks, be authentic, and practice leadership. I want my students to see themselves clearly — as respectable and evolving human beings. I facilitate creative learning by strengthening their art-making capacities while increasing their awareness of how cities work.

Who Knows the City?

The dictionary defines *knowledge* as "information, understanding, or skill that you get from experience or education; awareness of something" (Merriam-Webster Online 2015). It is critical to pay attention to the various kinds of knowledges — and knowledge systems — that are at play in classrooms and communities, and to affirm students and their families as knowledge bearers and knowledge creators. "Who knows?" is a simple, yet political question underlying this research. Sandra Harding (1987) writes that feminist methodologies question who can be a "knower." Harding recognizes that her theoretical claims exist within a historically patriarchal and racist educational system that has not valued the diversity of women's knowledges. Feminist methodologies ask questions that are relevant to women and girls who themselves are knowers and use knowledge to help improve their lives.

Building on Harding's assertions, I argue that children are knowers, too. They know things that are valuable for making cities more livable. However, youth knowledge — especially that of marginalized children — is rarely consulted to inform sound decision-making about infrastructural or cultural resources. Harding also specifies that there is no one universal woman's knowledge. The same is true of children: there is no one universal youth voice. A Brazilian saying, *Cada cabeça e um mundo (*Every mind is its own world) captures the epistemological impulse of learning — that everyone has their own truth — and by extension, that the diversity of our truths informs the greater whole. Just like classrooms, cities are diverse spaces that can benefit from understanding the specific living conditions and aspirations of its diverse residents.

Paulo Freire provides a philosophical precedent for valuing children's knowledge. He critiques the banking system of education, where knowledge is seen as deposited by teachers who know things into students who don't (1970). Harding's post-colonial feminist epistemologies and Freire's *Pedagogy of the Oppressed* provide a useful theoretical frame for participatory, arts- and culture-driven research with youth about living conditions in their communities. Freire notes that the act of study evokes an attitude toward the world that he sees as a confrontation (1985). EM provided a healthy confrontation with arts education and urban planning discourse on at least two levels. First, youth research on SRTS confronted the adult-driven emphasis of city planning. Second, the interdisciplinary nature of our work (combining hard facts, intuitive imagery, and personal stories) disrupted disciplinary boundaries in arts education and urban planning.

At a basic level, art is about telling a story — whether literal or fictional. Toni Morrison saw power in the act of giving voice to silenced stories (1990). EM expanded the range of stories that are told, read, seen, and heard to amplify perspectives on mobility held by Latino teenagers in LA's Eastside. Designer John Maeda recommends that we rethink the value of storytelling in leadership development. He argues, "A leader doesn't start with storytelling, they start with story listening" (2014). Compassionate leadership, just like thoughtful design or artmaking, provides an opportunity for people to listen better to each other. EM expanded opportunities for students to ask each other questions, to listen well, and to tell their stories to listeners who did not yet know them — including transportation decision-makers.

Mobility interviews. Photos: Author.

The Power of Voice

Students long to express themselves, be seen accurately, have their experiences valued, learn new things, and belong to a winning team. The pain of feeling voiceless, misunderstood, or presumed incompetent vexes the racist or sexist classroom. A social justice approach to arts education must do precisely the opposite — help students become the experts of their own representations, practice compassionate storytelling and story listening, and affirm the value of diverse identities, social conditions, and lived experiences.

It takes practice to learn to play an instrument, dance something choreographed, draw a portrait, or deliver a soliloquy. Students who have not had the chance to learn how to draw may grey their pages with erasures. Students who lack confidence in spelling or grammar may hover over a blank page with pencils frozen between their fingers — even if an assignment is given in free verse. Gloria Anzaldúa writes that healing can conjure back voices that have been socialized into silence. "*En boca cerrada no entran moscas* — 'Flies don't enter a closed mouth'" — she was told as a girl (1987, 76). Jacques Derrida suggested that the specter of invisibility must be confronted. He wrote, "One must see, at first sight, what does not let itself be seen. And this is invisibility itself" (1994, 3).

Children abound with creative ideas, impulses, and cultural assets, but, as Ken Robinson has noted, these tendencies are often stamped out of students instead of cultivated (2001). Students can be exposed to the arts and culture at home, in the neighborhood, or at school. A child's own autochthonous creative knowledge, grounded in their cultural identity and unique personality, is the root system for future artistic growth. We can fight invisibility by affirming youth voice and the rich connections between culture, identity, and art.

Seeing children as knowledge bearers instead of problems to solve is a first step towards creating an inclusive classroom culture ripe for creativity. Anzaldúa wrote about seeing and being seen as either a form of possession or a window for self-awareness:

> Seeing and being seen. Subject and object . . . The eye pins down the object of its gaze, scrutinizes it, judges it. A glance can freeze us in place; it can "possess" us. It can erect a barrier against the world. But in a glance lies awareness, knowledge. (1987, 64)

Awareness of misrepresentation or being seen by others in a negative light due to prejudice, was part of my cultural and political upbringing. My mother taught me about the "evil eye," and collected handmade amulets to protect her children from it. These wearable art works, stamped in metal, carved in red stone, or molded in blue glass, were designed to protect us from being injured by an outsider's negative gaze. It makes sense that I have worked as an educator to dispel potential for shaming, envy, or misrepresentation in the classroom by creating safe spaces where students can take risks, make mistakes, and demonstrate what they know and value. A child who sees herself as knowledgeable, can figure things out, and shape change will grow into an empowered adult.

Energy can also come from the process of invention itself. Noah Purifoy believed the process of making art was more powerful than any artworks created: "I am more concerned with the act of creating than I am with art itself. My primary concern is others getting into the act of doing something creative. Art is a tool to be used to discover the creative self" (Sirmans and Lipschutz 2015, 78). Importantly, Randy Martin suggests that making and performing art can activate participants to move from mere spectatorship to becoming political actors (Martin 1990, 1). Because of the lack of arts education in most urban schools, students can feel ill prepared to express the depth of their ideas through an unfamiliar medium. Helping students "get into the act" requires facilitating a culture of experimentation and positive risk-taking in the classroom that embraces failure as a part of the creative process.

For example, EM ninth graders eagerly choose one of the twelfth graders' beliefs to illustrate, but visualization was more challenging. Some students began drawing immediately, while less confident students hesitated. One young man glared so intently at his page that I thought he would burn an image into the paper with his eyes. "Let yourself begin," I whispered. "You can always make it better later." He nodded with relief. "I always do that," he said. "I stop myself." He finally relaxed and got into the act.

In EM, I varied the use of arts materials and performance techniques to emphasize process over product. Introducing printmaking welcomed new students to the joys of messy work. They liked moving around between the sketching, cutting, and printing phases of creation. This turned the classroom into a social laboratory for image making. I took a similar approach with writing students, using performance to build a culture of listening and speaking out. Facilitating a culture of experimentation in the classroom helps students face the empty page, the blank space, or silence with curiosity instead of trepidation about how to fill it. Artists face this challenge every day. We practice honing our craft through technique, but when it is time to create, we emphasize the process first. Only after creating a body of work do, we choose what we like best and what we don't during the editing, revising, and curation phases. We combined skill building through instruction with risk-taking in the creative process.

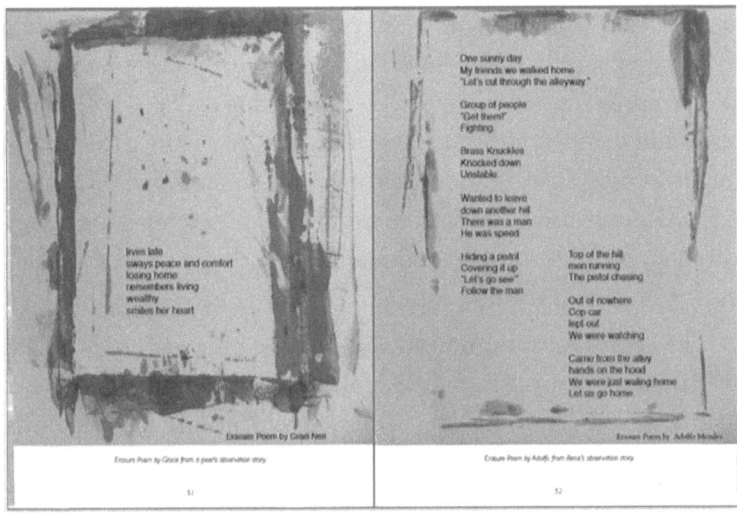

Erasure Poems. Photos: Author.

The Art of Knowing

The creative process is inherently driven by inquiry. In EM, our shared quest was to learn about the impact of mobility on students' lives through the creative process. Students expressed what they know and learned through visualization, physical and vocal performance, and digital tools. Local cultural, linguistic, and geographical assets affirmed students' knowledge and imaginations. Their art works were imbued with a sense of shared purpose, connection to regional histories, and invention of brighter futures.

The arts can be used to express, document, reframe, or critique human experiences and environments. Artmaking is a platform to practice the powers of self-definition, cultural preservation, and innovation. Classrooms could focus on any topic through multiple media. The arts are languages and systems for knowing, as much as they are content itself. They activate holistic learning that intersects facts with feelings and weds subjective and analytical ways of knowing. Artmaking offers outlets for students to express what they know, but

27

also, how they feel about what they know, what they want to know, and why they want to know it. A curriculum that incorporates feelings and perceptions strengthens student learning since cognition is a layered and complex process involving social and embodied language, thought, sensory perception, interpretation, and empathy (Kamenetz 2015). The arts provide a way to practice and develop proficiency in perceiving, communicating, and managing feelings — all valuable life skills for successful relationships and compassionate leadership.

The ability to communicate feelings and observations was central to EM. Safety is a pillar of SRTS and a topic about which ELARA students were experts, having witnessed violence on their way to or from school, or having lost family members to violence. The topic of safety could not have been adequately understood, or addressed, without students' stories and sentiments. Creative writing, drawing, and painting allowed the learning community to grasp the deeper ramifications of safety on students' lives. For example, violence was a central theme in students' observation stories. While one student told a humorous tale about a flock of chickens trying to cross the road, most of the observation stories were dominated by having witnessed violence. Reading the stories aloud in class generated empathy for each other and an awareness of the different risks facing males and females. Joel concluded, "Fear is a natural response and there's no shame in it, especially if the situation is very serious" (Shimshon-Santo 2015, 27). We brainstormed ways to increase safety through behavioral changes and by advocating for improved transportation infrastructure.

"Knowledge is power" is a common adage, but it is equally true that power restricts or expands knowledge. For example, while research has shown many benefits of arts education on student learning (Catterall, Dumais, and Hampden-Thompson 2012; Greenfader, Brouillette, and Farkas 2014; Shimshon-Santo 2010a, 2010b; Hanley and Noblit 2009), access to arts education reveals geographies of power, privilege, and exclusion across place, identity group, and socio-economic status (CREATE CA 2015). Investment in culturally relevant arts education during childhood expands the range of tools children can master to express themselves as creative thinkers, knowers, and makers. Preparing and encouraging students in creativity is an investment in the diversity of knowledge production and homegrown talent in cities.

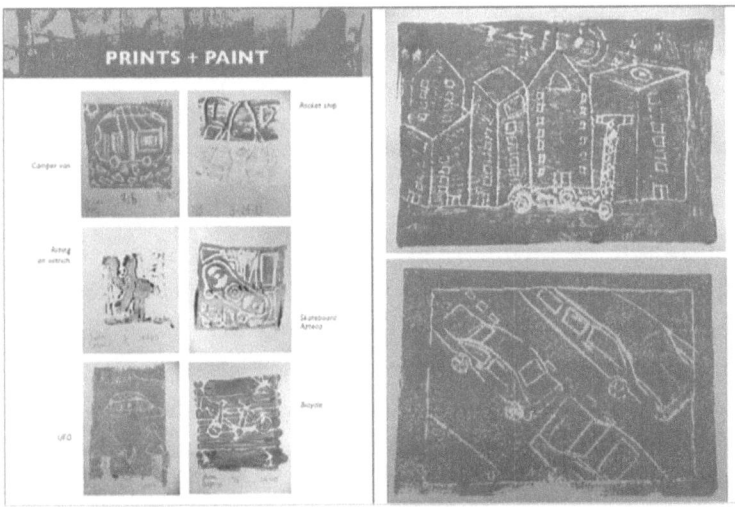

Printmaking about modes of transportation. Photos: Author.

HOW THE PROJECT UNFOLDED

Locale

ELARA is a public school with a formal urban planning and design focus on the Esteban Torres High School campus near Cesar Chavez Boulevard and Eastern Avenue on Los Angeles' Eastside. East Los Angeles is a creative mecca for Latine culture and ingenuity. The city's Latino roots reach down hundreds of years. East Los Angeles had become an intercultural crossroads molded in part by racial housing covenants limiting the ability of Latine, Asian American, African

American, and Jewish residents to purchase homes in areas of their choosing. According to current census data, East Los Angeles residents are now 92% Latino and 43% foreign born. One third of local residents are 18 or under. Neighborhood high school graduation rates are 46%, and just under 6% of local residents have completed an undergraduate degree (United States Census Bureau 2015). The community continues to organize to affirm local Latino identity and autonomy, support the well-being of its residents, and navigate the imposing pressures of gentrification (Masters 2012).

Approaching ELARA

On my way to ELARA, I pass the happiest ice cream shop in the world. Hand-painted on the doorway, in curly blue and green letters, are the words *Aqui pasan las mujeres mas bonitas del mundo* (The most beautiful women in the world pass through here). I veer under the crisscrossed freeway, over ramps, and turn right down a residential street lined with one-story, single-family homes. Parking in front of a house surrounded by a tall white metal gate, a neighbor's VATO LOCO Wi-Fi server finds my phone. I know that when the VATO LOCO Wi-Fi perceives my digital presence by popping up on my cell phone to request access, I have arrived.

There are no painted crosswalks or stop signs at this corner between the homes and the school. I wait for traffic to pass and run with my bag of art supplies and laptop bouncing up and down inside the sturdy orange bag woven from plastic thread that I purchased in Chiapas decades ago. With its simple, utilitarian construction it may outlive me. It is early morning. Students are scattered on the sidewalks and crossing the street, heading to A period.

A skateboarder wearing a green hoodie circles the sidewalk next to the fire hydrant at the school entrance. We smile and exchange hellos. We have often talked about active transportation. I've taken his photograph and a group portrait with his skateboarder crew. My team of student researchers has done the same thing with hundreds of other local youth. We've been talking to skateboarders, pedestrians, bike riders, and car drivers about how they get around. Students have taken photos and made charcoal drawings of crosswalks, sidewalks, buses, and trains. The youth research team has been drawing, writing, making prints, mapping routes to school online using Google tools, and making videos for YouTube for months. We even got dressed up and took the bus downtown to speak with the Los Angeles Metropolitan Transportation Authority (METRO LA) about youth perspectives on SRTS. Invite an artist-nerd-in-residence to teach at your school and people get to know each other.

I open the heavy door to the main office and greet the front staff. I sign the lined visitors notebook and my hand reaches for a fluorescent yellow visitor sticker.

"You don't need one of those," says the middle-aged woman at the front desk. "I know you." She smiles.

"Gracias Madre," I say. I realize how much I've enjoyed seeing her on the way in and out of the school this year. We talk *chisme.* She briefs me on upcoming events. She asks me for updates about the students' progress.

I push past the swinging door, walk through the administrative building, and out the back by the nurse's office. The corridors are jammed with teenagers. The river of youth is speckled with radiant hair dyes, selective piercings, and backpacks personalized with permanent ink pens.

"Dr. A!"

"Good morning! See you in class?"

"Yes!"

I have come to love this place.

31

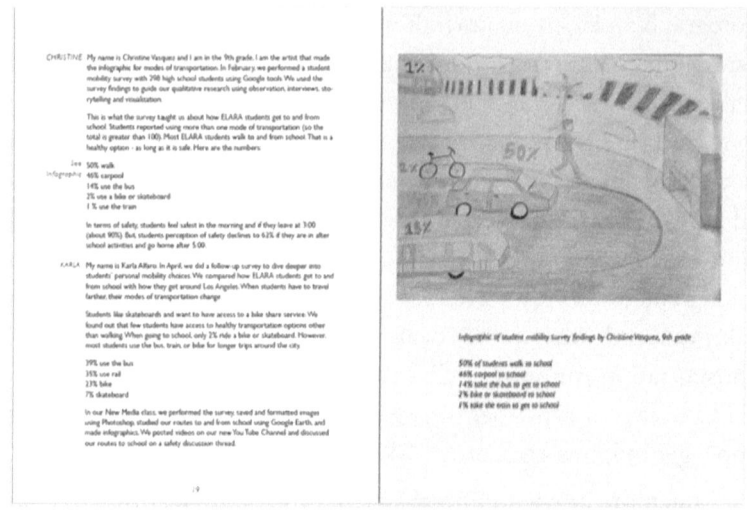

Student mobility survey findings & infographic.

Learning by Doing

We have accomplished a great deal since the first day I met Michael Rocha's journalism class. I have developed a routine for introductions since my name is difficult to pronounce. I tell them my long, multiethnic, hyphenated name, and offer them a simple option.

"Hello, my name is Dr. A," I say. "I'm an artist and a professor. I believe that college begins before you apply to the university. I'm here because I want you to graduate high school and come visit me, come study in college."

Throughout the EM project, we collected and analyzed quantitative and qualitative data on mobility. The team gained quantitative information from student mobility surveys to assess which modes of transportation students used to get to and from school, and their perceptions of safety. I presented the data to students to discuss in our arts classes. From the initial survey of over 200 students, we learned that 50% of ELARA students walked to school. Walking is a healthy way to get around if students feel safe. However, students' perceptions of safety declined significantly, from 90% at 8:00 a.m. to 62% after 3:00 p.m., when they returned home after school. This safety data was immediately significant for students, teachers, and administrators because the community regarded after-school activities as critical for college preparation, sports, and internships.

While biking or skateboarding are healthy choices, the survey revealed that only 2% of ELARA students biked or skateboarded to or from school. We discussed this finding in class, and students explained the reasons. Riding a bike to school made them targets for aggravated assault and theft, and bikes were often stolen from school during the day. Some teens didn't own a bike, or owned one that they were embarrassed to ride to school. Students determined that both safety and access to personal mobility devices influenced low bike ridership. Analysis revealed that many students preferred skateboarding to biking. Skateboards were associated with a positive youth lifestyle. Teens appreciated that they could leave their boards in the classroom, where they were less likely to be stolen than a bike.

The survey results provided a springboard to get students asking questions, thinking critically about SRTS, and making art. Student inquiry guided personal stories about epic walks to school, peer and parent interviews, photographs, drawings, paintings, prints, infographics, erasure poems, and digital maps. In EM research, stories were written, spoken, and conveyed through visual art. The interdisciplinary approach brought valuable qualities to the research. For example, in our modes of transportation studies, writers told personal stories from their own lives. We learned about cars that stopped for chickens that were trying to cross the road, and kids being mistaken for criminals and harassed by the police. Students remembered the sounds of punches smacking against someone's bent over jaw during a fight, and the weight of a sweat-drenched T-shirt after running home in fear.

Fine art students depicted both conventional and imagined modes of transportation. They visualized bikes, skateboards, buses, trains, and pedestrians, and invented ostrich rides, Aztec skateboards, floating buses, and UFOs. Interactions between disciplines, and across age groups, imbued our learning with playfulness and breadth. The ninth graders reminded me that kids are as interested in exploring the universe as they are in simply getting to and from school. Young people want the freedom to move about freely — in the city or the galaxy.

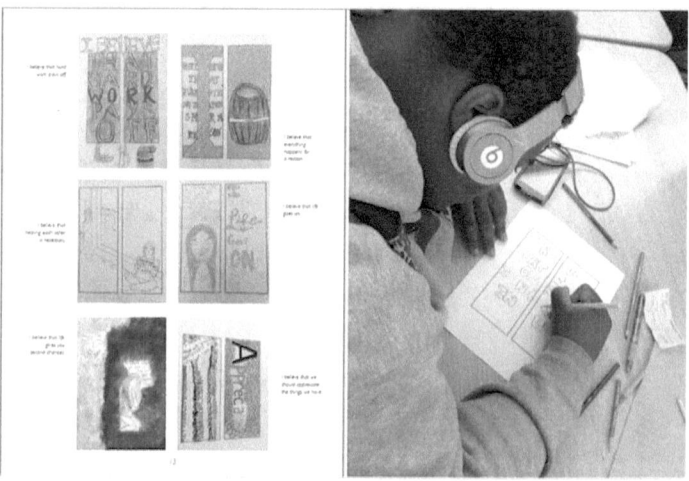

Archive of personal belief visualizations. Photos: Author.

One of the many EM arts activities I developed emphasized belief systems and overcoming adversity. It was inspired by the Edward R. Morrow *This I Believe* series, initiated during World War II. I asked students to write stories and poetry, and to draw based on their beliefs as a source of strength during challenging times like war or violence. Adolfo, a tall and athletic student, filled his pages with personal stories. He discussed being bullied in middle school and the impact it had on his health. His belief: "I believe that people can change:"

With the shock of my father deserting us, my mother could no longer keep track of my nutrition and I didn't care about what I was eating. As I became heavier people became meaner. At some point, I even began bullying myself. (Shimshon-Santo 2015, 11)

Adolfo used creative writing to reframe his transformation from a victim to a confident high school student who was graduation-bound. By the project's culmination, he described this activity as his favorite, because he got to know his peers on a deeper level and to respect them more.

Each student's story of overcoming an obstacle generated a shared pride in the group's resilience. One day, we studied a podcast by Elvia Bautista (2006) who had lost her brother to gang violence. A student called me over to talk. It was the one-year anniversary of her father's death from what she described as bad decisions. She chose to frame her story as a way that honored her deceased father. "I believe my dad is still with me even though he isn't really here anymore," she wrote (Shimshon-Santo 2015, 12). Helena, who shared a desk with her, used the activity to critique an abusive relationship. She wrote, "I believe that when a couple breaks up, they should respect each other and let go" (Shimshon-Santo 2015, 11). One student encouraged everyone to be grateful for their parents since he had almost lost his father during a raid by the Immigration and Customs Enforcement (ICE). He explained that he would not be in school today if his father had been taken from his family. Instead, he would be working full time to support his household. Another student emphasized second chances after she overcame childhood meningitis.

The twelfth-grade journalism students swapped their work with the ninth-grade visual arts students who chose favorite beliefs to illustrate. Sharing writing and imagery connected students across ages and disciplines. Students forged leadership beliefs and authority grounded in shared experiences, values, and aspirations.

Youth presentation at Metro LA headquarters.

As the project culminated, students analyzed their core findings, and rehearsed their presentation for the Metro LA headquarters. Rehearsal was critical for leadership development. As a retired choreographer, dance taught me the power of practice. We rehearsed until the movements were embedded in our sense memory and felt natural. Practice freed us to fill the form with our own identities and unique performance qualities. Students diligently rehearsed their message, pitch, and posture.

I collaborated with Tham Nyugen and Lisette Covarrubias in Metro LA's Active Transportation office to facilitate an intergenerational exchange between students and Metro professionals. Adults were selected for cultural competencies and leadership qualities that celebrated *Latinidad*, immigrant experiences, identities as first-generation college goers, and Eastside residents. The exchange began with a panel of adult transportation professionals and concluded with the EM youth research presentation. The transportation experts inspired the students to aspire to college and a professional career that could shape the city. The youth impressed the adults with their artworks, infographics, stories, mobility analysis, preparation, and confidence.

Lisette Covarrubias asked the EM team, "What is preventing students from moving through their own environment?" Students talked about safety and their experiences of active transportation. They requested increased service during peak hours (when students are on their way to or from school), since buses filled to capacity were leaving students on the curb. They advocated for better street lighting, so when they walked home at night, they would feel safer. They wanted painted crosswalks to deter automobile collisions with pedestrians. They asked how to reduce speeding and hit-and-runs near schools and requested shaded bus stops. They explained that many students don't have access to bikes or skateboards and requested that Metro locate a bike-share service on the Eastside. They advocated for free or affordable transit passes for low-income students.

The hearty debate demonstrated that EM prepared youth as leaders able to speak authoritatively about their vision for SRTS in the neighborhood. Students trusted their ideas because they were grounded in rigorous group research informed by multiple methods. A blogger from Metro, who attended the event and was enthusiastic about the students, wrote:

> The city being built now is the city that they're probably going to live in for the next few decades — so it makes sense they'd want to know about the process of how it's being changed and have some say in what's going on. Hopefully they were able to take away some useful information from Metro — and vice versa! And who knows? In a few years, maybe these high

schoolers will be the ones calling the shots in shaping Los Angeles. (Chen 2015)

We then prepared to share stories through public testimony (i.e., an Open Mic) and an eBook Launch at the school library. While practicing for the Open Mic, Edwin faced his peers with a serious look and said, "My fellow Americans." Everyone laughed, including him. I saw this as a form of role-play as he defined his own leadership style.

Nadine expressed her pride in participation and "voicing the voice:"

> In this whole experience, I got to know how we can involve each other in our community…Everyone stood up and expressed themselves and the spotlight was on them. It made me open up and realize that we are individual people. I am proud to see that teenagers can voice the voice and be heard." (Public Testimony 2015b)

Yakeline was shy to take her turn at the microphone. She summoned her courage and said, "If we want change in our community, we have to get out there and let them know what we would like" (Public Testimony 2015a). The once-timid student received rousing applause from her peers.

Esteban described what he learned as something new and memorable:

> The process…was pretty hard at times. But, in the end, it was all worth it. To go up on stage in front of the podium and talk with the people from Metro and tell them our experience of this (SRTS). It was…once in a lifetime and really fun. (Public Testimony 2015b).

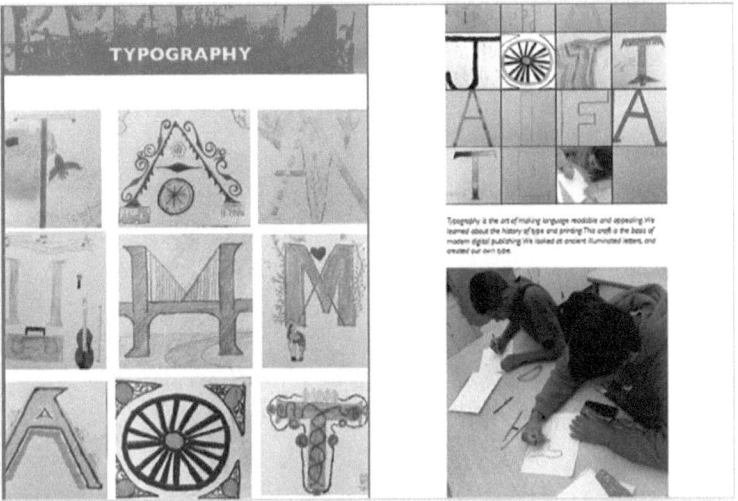

Typography studies. Photos: Author.

On the last day, students and teachers gathered in the school library. John Lee and his students displayed EM book spreads they had mounted on poster board. With a few clicks, students downloaded the publication and archived it in the school library alongside other published writers and artists. Students scrolled through the publication online, smiling and pointing at their contributions and favorites.

Students discussed what they did and learned in an Open Mic session. The teachers spoke about student achievements with pride. The twelfth graders described their experiences with words like *work* and *belonging*. "I am a member of #ElaraMoves," began many of the student testimonies. The ninth graders had chosen seats in the back rows. After seeing the seniors brave the microphone, they came forward to speak and be heard. Then there were handshakes, hugs, photos snapping, and trays of sandwiches to be eaten. Students left the library that day as published authors, exhibited artists, and emerging urban experts on mobility in the city.

Student video and social media generation. Photos: Author.

CONCLUSION

The EM project synthesized arts and design education with urban studies, while investing in students as emerging leaders. Students cultivated leadership through inquiry that exercised their intellectual and creative capacities. They created original art, and developed skills in editing, curating, rehearsing, performing, and publishing. Students shared their knowledge across distinct settings — from downtown skyscrapers to their own neighborhood. The research process revealed that youth have valuable urban expertise, and that their visions, opinions, and imaginations can help inform more inclusive and livable cities.

Studying mobility provided the groundwork for intergenerational connections between the high school students, higher education, and city agencies in the area. A focus on the city inspired students and teachers alike. Karla, an enthusiastic ninth grader, became an urban advocate in her drawing class. She wrote:

> It's great talking about transportation in the city, because in our city people mostly use cars. This is the reason why we have

so much pollution and smog. I think other schools should also start focusing on the city more because . . . you could actually realize that there is a lot wrong with it and that we can try to fix it together. (Shimshon-Santo 2015, 16)

English teacher Michael Rocha claimed that the project helped his students see themselves as change makers:

This project pushed students to . . . to investigate current issues in their community and become agents of change. As our students interviewed their peers and their families they gave voice to the challenging nature of life on the Eastside; they honored those voices by proposing changes to the community. (Shimshon-Santo 2015, 5)

"Being a part of ELARA Moves was a natural fit," wrote New Media teacher Hector Verduzco. "Students used Google Earth to map their routes and analyze safety concerns they have on a daily basis" (Shimshon-Santo 2015, 5). Design teacher John Lee was pleased with the college preparatory focus that helped his students prepare for future careers in the arts and design.

This study suggests that arts education can generate qualitative and spatial knowledge for understanding cities and activating communities. The project's scale influenced a school culture by sparking creative learning across multiple disciplines and grade levels in both arts and non-arts-based classrooms. EM generated, studied, and influenced local knowledge about a key urban system—transportation —by engaging youth and amplifying their voices with decision makers.

Connecting the Dots

I wrote this essay after collaborating for three years with regional community arts and popular education activists in Canada, Mexico, Nicaragua, and Panama. At the time, I was directing an arts education program in a public university in California that prepared student artists to teach, and connected high school students and their families to the college. Writing this challenged me to reflect on our process, and to present insights from our work to people from different places who may have never been to Los Angeles. The program, called ArtsBridge, taught lesson planning, child development, and classroom ecology to university fellows, while offering year-round instruction in visual art, design, media arts, dance, architecture, music, and drama to students in Los Angeles, Compton, Lynwood, and Santa Monica. We worked closely with classroom teachers and district representatives to make this all happen. This essay introduces readers to our local context then shares stories from dance education classrooms and media studies classrooms. We found that dance education supported critical thinking, challenged gender stereotypes, and transmitted cultural knowledge. In media studies, technology and design were used to affirm students' bilingual language and cultural assets while reducing the digital divide.

FROM DENDRITES TO REGIONAL ECOLOGIES

Long before Los Angeles became famous for the Hollywood movie industry, it was home to the Tongva Nation. In the 1700s, the region was colonized by an intercultural group of Mexican settlers who named it El pueblo de nuestra señora la reina de los ángeles del rio de porciúncula (The Town of Our Lady the Queen of the Angels on the River Porciuncula). By 1781, the city was home to people of African, Native American, and European descent. In fact, the first city census verified that many residents were a mixture of more than one cultural group, and half of the residents were of African, or part African, descent. [1]

How would you tell someone about your neighborhood if they had never seen it, or had only heard stereotypes about its people or place? Contemporary depictions of Los Angeles have been constructed in the global imagination through television, films, magazines, and lyrics that venerate or denigrate this place and the people who live here. On the ground, Los Angeles is many things to many people—nearly four million people who live in the city proper and approximately ten million who live in the county. While Los Angeles is a recognized global hub for cultural and artistic production, it is also a blatantly unequal place to live. The economic disparities here would rival the greatest cinematic production in their dramatic force.

Depending on where you are, Los Angeles can feel like an international gathering place for families and trade. Los Angeles is not easily understood in its entirety—even for residents who live somewhere in the city's 500-square-mile radius. There is simply too much to see and know, and we are constantly changing.[2]

The ArtsBridge program I directed at UCLA's School of the Arts and Architecture in Los Angeles created educational pathways in the arts by fostering ongoing close contact between public schools in under-invested neighborhoods and universities. Given the geographic sprawl of Los Angeles, this is no simple feat. The university is bunkered by the affluent neighborhoods of Beverly Hills, Bel Air, and Brentwood while partnership schools were primarily in the South, Central, Eastern areas of Los Angeles and the valley. To fulfill the immediate potential of direct college access for secondary students, one of my first decisions was to emphasize high school collaborations. Our first partner high school was David Starr Jordan High School in Watts. In the 1900s, Watts was a transportation nexus nicknamed "the hub of the universe." The Central Avenue jazz district in South Los Angeles was a place that nourished African American musicians and contributed to jazz innovation. I cite this example of cultural and place based assets to convey my view that the connectivity in our expanded circle of participants was mutually beneficial creatively and educationally.

History is the backdrop for a contemporary analysis of educational and social justice. Immediately relevant to our work was how privilege and discrimination were engraved into the city's geography through settler colonization, racist restrictive housing covenants, exclusionary educational policy, and the carcel system. The court case *Plessy v. Ferguson* (1896) solidified white privilege in education by declaring racial segregation a national legal precedent. Racial segregation was formally sanctioned in education for sixty years. While the landmark case *Brown v. Board of Education of Topeka* (1954) rendered desegregation legally unconstitutional, the significant role Mexican Americans played in challenging school segregation is lesser known. Eight years earlier, the *Mendez v. Westminster* (1946) case found that Mexican American student's Fourteenth Amendment rights were being violated by Mexican-only Schools. Mendez was the first successful case to successfully question the constitutionality of segregation.[3] Despite the formal reversal of legal segregation in 1954 (over a century after the *Plessy* case) Los Angeles schools remain de facto segregated by class, place, race, and nativity. The lack of parity in primary and secondary schooling spills into higher education and careers. By planting and tending to an ecology of connection between secondary schools and college, we used the power of proximity, communication, and care to cultivate a regional teaching and learning community.

I developed curricula on campus specifically for teaching artists, or ArtsBridge Scholars, who earned academic scholarships to design and facilitate arts education residencies in their genre at a school. Their diverse interests ranged from spoken word to painting, hip hop to Polynesian dance, and dramatic arts to architectural design. By facilitating a group cohort, we made space for creative, intellectual, and professional growth among the arts educators. Simultaneously, we facilitated access to on-campus and off-campus resources for youth, classroom teachers, and administrators. This included field trips, exhibitions, and performances for youth, teacher-in-service programs for classroom educators, and summer arts institutes for high school students. Thomas Turner, lead teacher at George Washington Carver Middle School, compared our regional learning community to "growing dendrites," or transmitting nerve synapses, in the body. [5] Mr. Turner's biological metaphor explains the connections that flourish in an inspired educational ecosystem.

We committed to getting to know each other and our different learning communities; becoming available and accessible to each other; being honest, diligent, and patient with each other; and taking creative risks. By cultivating a reliable interactive ecology, we were able to more easily share knowledge and leverage to circulate.

TRANSFORMATION AND BORDER CROSSING

One might ask, "what constitutes political action and how does arts education connect personal and social change?" The feminist movement, the civil rights movement, and the environmental movement have argued that sexism, racism, and environmental degradation are reproduced through historically constructed political, economic, and social institutions. However, each of these social movements has also recognized that personal action can be political. The reproduction of oppression is undergirded by negative misrepresentations of marginalized people and places. In contrast, the power of self-definition through creative expression allows creators to imagine themselves and the world in more accurate and empowering ways. An education that affirms cultural reclamation sparks personal changes in consciousness that are the seeds for larger social, economic, and institutional change.

One example of border-crossing is illustrated in work with students and teachers at George Washington Carver Middle School who created a play called *Welcome to the Border Now Go Back Where You Came From*. Their play was developed with teaching artist Lee Sherman of the Center Theater Group in collaboration with humanities teacher Thomas Turner. Techniques from the Brazilian theater activist Augusto Boal's Legislative Theater were used to create a play about immigration and educational justice. The students' play included a powerful tableau with a line of teenagers grasping arms to form an impenetrable wall of bodies that stretched the width of the auditorium. The youth wore block letters strung around their necks that spelled out the word b-o-r-d-e-r. The first time this tableau appeared in the play, it represented the United States-Mexico border. A young actor, playing the role of an immigrant, called out "Ayúdenme!" (Help me!) as they attempted to pry open the wall and cross over. "Está dificil!" (It's hard to!), the actors forming the wall replied in brash unison, their heads hanging down. In a subsequent scene, the youth resurrected the border tableau again, to represent the border to higher education. First, an actor playing the role of "undocumented student" moved successfully through primary and secondary school with high grades. "Congratulations!" her teachers said, as she received diplomas for excelling at each phase of her studies. But, after high school, the wall reappeared again on stage. "Ayúdenme!," the undocumented student called out as a placard reading "college" was held above the heads of the border tableau. As she tried unsuccessfully to cross the border into higher education the actors yelled back "Está dificil!" while she struggled to progress.

At the end of the play, the cast welcomed questions and answers from the audience. One classroom teacher asked the ensemble, "Now that you have made a play about immigrant student rights, how will you change legislation for undocumented students?" Silence filled the auditorium. Was it enough to create an educational tool that drew attention to the topic without proposing tangible changes? Clearly not. At this opportune moment I was able to be an open door rather than a barrier to the university. I praised the students for their work and invited the young actors to perform their play at the university, and to meet with immigrant student activists on campus who have been formative in changing legislation for undocumented students through Assembly Bill 540 (AB 540) and the Dream Act. George Washington Carver Middle School, the Center Theater Group, and ArtsBridge collaborated to present the play on campus, welcomed the students with a university tour, and held a roundtable discussion with student leaders about AB 540. Participants learned that undocumented students can indeed attend university in California and pay local tuition because of this legislation.

The positive impact of the collaboration was instantaneous and mutual. University students were pleased to meet and mentor teenagers who were asking the hard questions regarding educational access for undocumented youth. The teenagers were inspired by the activism of undocumented university students who overcame tremendous odds to pursue their dreams. Classroom teachers, teaching artists, and school administrators who were unaware of the AB 540 legislation learned about options for undocumented students and could better advise parents and future students. Finally, the performance and roundtable made it clear to participants how social change happens—through consistent dedicated effort over time. Everyone present, children and adults alike, rededicated themselves to the struggle to increase educational opportunities for undocumented students through awareness and action.

Another example of the connection between personal and social change can be felt during our participatory evaluation process. We evaluated the program with time together in each other's communities, focus groups, and preliminary and post surveys to analyze our progress. During on campus focus groups, we invited teenagers from South Los Angeles into university boardrooms along with school district representatives, classroom teachers, university students and staff. This participatory process reinforced the core values of intergenerational and intercultural connections. The evaluation process strengthened my view that having intergenerational participation at the table for decision-making enhances the perspectives available to the group and increases the likelihood that we can understand and respond to a more inclusive "truth."

One case in point involved a young dancer named Ulysses with a radiant smile and a shaved head who had participated in the dance program at Lynwood High School. While school and district administrators described the value of the program in terms of educational standards achieved, he offered feedback that focused the entire group on its higher purpose. "ArtsBridge helps students find their true self," he scrawled in blue ink on the whiteboard. His opinion became our guiding force for evaluation. In fact, we found that the most dramatic, quantifiable impact the program had was on increasing participants' positive views of themselves and their peers. We evaluated our progress through logic modeling, surveys, and regional performances and gatherings that we later wrote about and shared. [6]

Feeling good about oneself and one's community matters, especially for people in places who are consistently misrepresented, or left out of regional decision making processes. Learning to value ourselves and others is a crucial precursor to creating mutually beneficial relationships that connect communities, schools, and universities.

CURRICULUM AND CULTURAL REINVENTION

Together, we addressed cultural reclamation and reinvention by developing culturally affirming learning opportunities and curricula. Cynthia Wennstrom, a visual artist of Filipino and Anglo descent, made sense of the cross-cultural dimensions of her experience through poetry:

I come from a people who grow bananas and potatoes.

I study in a university where people frolic in country club beauty.

I teach young people who want to dance in their own skins.

I work with teachers who care about picking up the phone.

I bring to ArtsBridge an open cup.

I bring to my classroom pieces of a puzzle.[7]

Alicia Paniagua taught a Salsa in the Americas curriculum she developed for Millikan Middle School students who were enrolled in English Language Learning (ELL) classes. Her aim was to inspire young bilingual students through her own example. Paniagua energized her teaching with her three passions: salsa dancing, Spanish language, and Latin American studies. Salsa instruction provided an important creative outlet for ELL students who were regularly denied access to an arts elective. The experience also promoted Latine cultural and language assets within the school.

Teacher Kori Hamilton coached Iliana Phirippidis and Jena McRae to teach drama and language arts. They found that students better understood class reading when they analyzed it through dramatic play. For example, students read Laura Esquivel's novel *Like Water for Chocolate* (*Como Agua Para Chocolate*) and researched popular recipes from their own families. They then dramatized these recipes in skits and short videos such as "The Taco King" and "Daddy's Famous French Fries." This enriched the students' understanding of academic literature by relating it to their own lives and helped them rehearse the important leadership skills of group cooperation and public speaking.

Healing also took place when students were encouraged to include personal reflections in their artistic productions. For example, Tameka Norris developed a residency she titled Finding Meaning in College-Bound Words through Visual Art. Students in her class ferreted out words that high school students are tested on for college entrance examinations, but rarely hear in everyday English. As the students studied elaborate words, and represented their meaning in paintings, the images they painted evoked real-life stories from each young person's life. Norris explained how her art classes at Jordan High School regularly evoked cathartic stories and tears among her students. "I feel that the most powerful and authentic works came from . . . allowing a story to emerge from the medium," wrote Norris.[8] Safe spaces for reflection and healing grew inside her arts classroom.

Norris's art class created space for students to reveal the issues that impacted their lives and ability to succeed in school. One student in particular who had difficulty attending class consistently covered the background of her painting in black. Norris interpreted this student's work in the following way:

> Two red hearts floated at the upper and lower corners of the canvas. The upper heart was free and full, while the other lower heart was confined behind bars with a lock with no key. [The student] offered in critique that her boyfriend is in jail and probably will be for many years to come. She attends court hearings, knows all the court jargon and does what she can to help him stay in good spirits. Additionally she has seven siblings that she has to get ready for school daily.[10]

These examples demonstrate how creativity is a healing tool for personalizing curriculum. Creativity offers social and personal benefits to enjoy and find deeper meaning in schooling By the end of the four-year collaboration with Hamilton's classroom, at least four of her students were college bound. One headed straight to UCLA as an undergraduate, continued on complete graduate studies, and became a professional counselor supporting future generations. Hamilton went on to become a researcher and national advocate for equity in education. Norris (Artist T.J. Dedeaux-Norris) has become an accomplished visual and performance artist and professor of Art.

Historically, "informal" learning normally takes place in the home or neighborhood, while "formal" learning takes place in school. Informal learning often recognizes cultural knowledge that formal schooling may undervalue or even omit. Since knowledge is tied to power, affirming different epistemologies and ontologies (ways of knowing and worldviews) is a significant outcome of culturally affirming education.

We committed ourselves to bridging informal and formal learning by validating culturally grounded knowledge gained outside of school while also fulfilling formal requirements for study. One example of this took place when a middle school student at Millikan Middle School made vivid connections between her life at school and in her community through a visual arts exercise in collage with Cynthia Wennstrom. The student artists used strips of color that reminded her of a bird's wings and nearly flew off the page. Jasmine's artwork was inspired by a freedom song she sang in church on weekends. After telling the story of how she felt while singing that song in church, she sang the same song out loud to her teacher and classmates. In that moment, a young woman who had been struggling with reading and writing reclaimed her dignity by demonstrating she was a powerful communicator through song and image. Her role in the classroom shifted when she could finally be known for her strengths. Overall, after six months of visual arts study, this middle school Directed Reading and Writing classroom improved its language skills on comprehensive tests from grade three to grade six levels. The classroom teacher, and the school vice principal, Leah Bass-Bayliss, attributed this improvement directly to studying art because no other change had been made to their instructional plan.

Another example of how artmaking inspired spiritual empowerment took place in a sculpture class facilitated by Karen Huang and classroom teacher Alix Fournier at John Muir Middle School. Students wrote stories about imaginary creatures with special powers and then brought them to life in clay. Many of the pieces had deep spiritual significance to youth. Ramona, an eighth grader, made a sculpture she called the *Moses of Love*. She explained, it is "a symbol of luck because it likes to help people with their problems." Her creation that "only helps people who are nice and not mean," included a spherical form containing a sequined heart with an eye in its center, rabbit ears, wings, and a snake-like tail. Through her sculpture, Ramona invented an art piece that conveyed her desire for power over her daily life.

Akeba Jackson, a partner teacher at Dorsey High School, told the story of a high school student who complained when he was removed from her drama class that was replaced with a computer course. He told the counselor, "I need drama." "No you don't," the counselor rebuked. "You need computers." "No," the students said. "I need drama." The young man explained to me that they talk about emotions in Ms. Jackson's drama class. He also added, "My teacher does not have to care about me when school gets out at 3:05, but she does. She is not even my family, but she cares, and that makes me want to work that much harder." His response raises a crucial point. A quality education is a sensate experience that must cultivate the whole person including one's values, mind, body, and emotions.

Movement Literacy

Different artistic mediums activate specific "literacies" that are comparable in importance to the more recognized areas of writing, reading, or computation. Movement education involves embodied knowledge. The legacy of Cartesian thinking still undergirds many scholastic programs that fail to acknowledge that learning involves complex connections between the mind, body, and emotions. Not surprisingly, it is common to encounter difficulties gaining support for dance education among school administrators and teachers. Dance education fosters corporeal learning that requires putting one's own body on the line for learning. One's body becomes the artistic medium itself—the palette and the page.

The process of dance choreography and presentation can also become a forum for social analysis, public commentary, and public debate. A dance theater piece choreographed by Jordan High School students, under the guidance of classroom teacher Monzell Corley, was set to the music of Michael Jackson's well-known music video *Thriller*. However, the students structured their own version of *Thriller* set in a local public hospital. Martin Luther King / Drew Medical Center Hospital, then nicknamed "Killer King" by residents, was cited for serious deficiencies in care that threatened patients' lives. Ironically, the struggling hospital was built with the hopes of serving the community and named after the noted civil rights leader Dr. Martin Luther King Jr. and Dr. Charles Richard Drew, a path-breaking African American medical scientist. Through the dance performance, current events normally relegated to newspaper columns became points of discussion at school.

Youth presented their choreography on Halloween for the school community to the infectious sounds of a classic music video. Dancers playing patients were heaped in piles on the floor as they wallowed in pain and then rose to dance to a compelling beat as mummies and ghouls. Movements included a doctor/dancer ripping a fake baby from another performer's belly and throwing it across the stage irreverently. Both the creative and performative processes that invigorated the dance composition fostered critical thinking about the quality of social services in South Los Angeles through the language of dance. Student enthusiasm for learning was demonstrated through their work on a significant public health issue.

In the United States, legislation exists that stipulates equitable access to physical education for both boys and girls. An outcome of the women's movement, Title IX was passed in 1972 and requires gender equity for boys and girls including access to higher education, athletics, career education, education for pregnant and parenting students, among other areas. The core legislation states,

No person in the United States shall, on the basis of sex, be excluded from participation in, be denied the benefits of, or be subjected to discrimination under any education program or activity receiving federal financial assistance. [11]

Access to dance education in Los Angeles had fallen into a chasm between fine arts and physical education mandates—a problem that was then exacerbated by the lack of a Californian dance teaching credential. Since that time, California has reinstated dance teaching credentials, and the region is finding ways to grow preservice programs for dance teacher development and placement.

Gender stereotypes continue to limit access to movement expression for girls and boys. One vivid example took place in a high school where a school district was trying to implement their first dance education progam. The district chose to focus on secondary dance training through physical education. The initial response from the school was that dance could only be taught to girls because boys would reject the opportunity. Ninth-grade girls would be offered dance while ninth-grade boys would study weight training. The school quietly permitted unequal standards of participation when ninth-grade boys weren't allowed to dance, and girls weren't encouraged to lift weights during their first year of high school. Our program decided to only collaborate with the school district if dance education was offered to both boys and girls. This experience allowed us to challenge outdated gender roles about who wants to dance. While our position on dance as a coeducational activity was initially seen as confrontational, the school quickly warmed up to the idea of boys dancing when they saw the program in action. By the end of the dance residency, the physical education (PE) director, who was also the school's football coach, became convinced that dance could be offered for both boys and girls. In a communal electronic journal, he wrote:

> [We] were enthralled with today's dance. I think many of the students, particularly boys, felt much more relevance to this [hip hop] movement because it's something they see every day. Today showed me what I believed but needed to see. Dance on any campus can be big. [12]

Dance is also a valuable forum for teaching cultural studies. Desiree Gallardo taught Hawaiian and Polynesian dance forms for students to gain a new respect for Pacific Island culture and values while making connections with their own family backgrounds. Gallardo explains,

> Not only did they learn how to do the steps, but they learned how to spell the names of each step that I taught them— *kaholo*, *kalakaua*, *hela*, and *uehe*. . . . These exercises make connections of sound through spelling the Hawaiian language and listening to two different hula music/dance styles. [13]

These examples demonstrate how schools benefited from including dance education as an academic subject. Whether embodying social commentary, enhancing gender equity, or learning cultural history through movement, dance education catalyzed understanding of identity, culture, history, and society.

MEDIA STUDIES

Media literacy is a crucial skill for youth who are bombarded with media messages but do not always learn how to critique them or to author their own. Understanding media and technology is enhanced by basic knowledge of design and visual art concepts. A residency at David Starr Jordan High School connected geometry teacher Bill Branscomb to Audrey Ma and Erin Jacobs who introduced his tenth-grade students to basic spatial design concepts and computer skills. Students created collages of their lives that used text and imagery to create media messages about what they valued. Students chose to focus on recent mass mobilizations for immigrant rights, the importance of steadfast friends, the tragedy of Hurricane Katrina, the importance of staying connected to one's cultural roots, and anxieties about transitioning from childhood into adulthood. Mr. Branscomb was impressed by the creativity that flowed from his students. He compared student learning through design to ripening grapes on the vine.

Introductory design studies were linked to college preparation when three design students were invited to continue their studies at the university Summer Design Institute. Scholarships were provided by the Summer Programs Office for high school students to study music video and game design in college. Rogelio Acevedo, education coordinator at the Watts Towers Arts Center near the high school, hosted a college arts orientation for students and families before they studied at the university.

Despite the positive overall experience, obstacles did need to be overcome. Initially, no female high school students applied for the scholarship since girls were not given the same liberties by their parents as their male counterparts. Special attention was required to encourage girls participation by close conversations with their guardians.

Also, bringing students together on campus did not blur the existence of privilege and economic inequality. In her exit interview, high school student Sonia Balonas commented that the other students were familiar with the advanced programs while she had never seen them before. She was slowed down by having to aimlessly press random buttons on the computer screen to decipher the functions while her peers seemed to navigate through the program having had prior experience. Thankfully, the following year a nonprofit organization, the Media Aid Center under the direction of Martin Cheeseborough, brought a fully functional media lab to her school. Efforts like these can close the digital divide.

Despite the challenges, students showed tenacity, created original work, experienced college life, and earned college credit that would reflect well on future university applications. "I always wanted to learn how to make video games," explained David Scoggins, "and I got tired of people telling me I couldn't do something." After making her own music video, Balonas said,

> I learned that I never knew I could get so nervous under pressure and around strangers. I never knew I could be so shy. I learned that it doesn't really matter . . . if you have not done it before. If you apply yourself, you really try, and once in a while ask for help, you can get anything done. [14]

Balonas's parents were supportive and pleased with her university summer studies. "We need more programs like this to give opportunities," Mr. Balonas said. The family invited me to celebrate her coming of age in a *quinceañera* celebration later that summer, which was an impressive event. Editing and directing a music video, experiencing college life, and celebrating her transition into young adulthood, all contributed to her important rites of passage. [15]

At the time, LAUSD documented 93 different languages spoken by their student body. However, the overwhelming majority of bilingual LAUSD students are Spanish speakers. A champion for bilingual education, Professor Kris Gutierrez raises the important point that every student who studies English, whether it is their first language or not, is an English-language learner. [16] The official terminology used to designate bilingual students reflects the heated discourse about bilingual education in a state that all too often depicts bilingual or polyglot students from a deficiency perspective rather than an asset-based perspective. The bilingual education movement, in many ways inspired by the Chicano and immigrant rights movements, continues to advocate for the value of bilingualism as a useful skill set rather than a problem.

In California public schools, students who are not reading and writing at grade level, were introduced to English later in life, or live in households where English is not the dominant tongue are often placed in ELL classes and required to study English twice a day at the expense of other subject areas such as science or the arts. As a result, many ELL students are systematically denied the opportunity to study dance, music, drama, or art. Ironically, in the effort to increase English language instructional hours students are denied creative outlets for literacy development through the arts.

Laurel Bybee created a design curriculum for middle school students in eighth-grade history and for students assigned to an ELL class. Working with a middle school ELL class, Bybee developed three activities that introduced students to the environment of Adobe Illustrator. First, she instructed students in typography by learning about font families and constructing a font family tree affirming their design skills along with their own genealogy and geographical origin. The second assignment introduced students to the camera and created original self-portraits. Finally, their typography skills and portraits were used to create bilingual posters in English and their language of origin. The creative student work highlighted their bilingualism as communications and cultural assets. The bilingual posters were an outlet for students to represent themselves to the larger school community on their own terms visually and linguistically.

CONNECTING THE DOTS

Oscar Neal, a Jordan High School alum and Watts community leader, described our community-building as "connecting the dots." For Neal, border crossing within our city's educational system would change the map of our lives, converting tiny "dots" on an urban grid to relationships between real people and places. He explained to a gathering of community partners from across the city,

> If I look around the circle here we are beginning to connect the dots. . . . It is very important to understand that we all have an obligation and a duty to give back . . . and in doing that will fulfill some of the things of our life ambition. [17]

Cultural connections pulse through the bloodlines and stories of Los Angeles' residents. At a gathering with regional arts education and popular educators, I met a young man at UniTierra (University of the Land) in Chiapas whose father had left the area to find alternative employment in the United States. He explained that his father's departure pained him, and he had temporarily lost his ability to speak and move his arm. Slowly, he overcame his silence, and was now able to share his story publicly. I had traveled by plane, car, and foot to visit

UniTierra while his father might be living or working next door to me in Los Angeles. The earth and water are borderless, and our families are too. Resilient family ties can be sustained across migrations if we value and tend to our connections. I could never begin to understand the city of Los Angeles without understanding how the city's threads are woven into the very fabric of our broader global landscape.

Arts Education for the Next Generation of Culture Makers

Long before sticky-sweet, rainbow-colored candy came to represent the vulnerability of Black children to racist violence and murder, my daughter wrote a play called "The History of Evil Skittles." She was seven. At the time, Trayvon Martin was a year younger, in the first or second grade. She wrote the play when theater makers came to her school to teach children how to write their own scripts. Students created worlds and narrated what happened inside them. Arts education became a platform for students to talk about difficult things. The children's plays were performed before a packed crowd of all ages in the school cafetorium. Moments like these, when communities gather to witness and celebrate the creativity of children, affirm their immense potential. Safe, affirming spaces for learning are critical for children's flourishing.

Born and raised in California, I was educated in public schools, as were my children. I'm from an immigrant family that is intercultural and interfaith: Jewish, Black, Ifa, Brazilian. Our journeys to the U.S. came through Africa, South America, the Middle East and Europe. Cultures that don't often coexist found a home inside ours. First generation on my mother's side, and second generation on my father's, my parents also attended public schools in the Middle East and the U.S. My paternal grandfather told me that it was against the law for Jewish children to attend public schools. At the time, Jewish boys were educated at the Rabbi's home, but education was gender segregated with no options for girls. Marginalized families from distinct cultures have experienced obstacles, often more severe. The slave codes codified in law forbade African-descended people from studying in the U.S. The lack of access to a culturally affirming education denigrates self worth and reproduces social inequality. Poet Nikky Finney wrote, "the ones who longed to read and write, but were forbidden, who lost hands and feet, were killed by laws written by men who believed they owned other men."

The fate of our children balances on top of this historical frame. Nobel Prize winner Toni Morrison wrote that "our race-inflected culture not only exists, it thrives. The question is whether it thrives as a virus or a bountiful harvest of possibilities."

Reimagining and reinvesting in public education is critical for any society to move forward. I've come to believe that we will never achieve the lofty aims of participation, belonging and democracy without reimagining our culture. Arts education, when dedicated to multiplicity and inclusion, can help us learn from the past and imagine who we wish to become.

Positive connections between home, neighborhood and school make a difference in children's lives. I've witnessed this vividly during arts and cultural activities in school. When my son's second-grade class drew imaginary passports to visit the African Savanna to study the ecosystem of the rhinoceros, his desire to learn was ignited by wanting to know more about where his father's ancestors hailed from. During this activity, students studied science, geography, language arts and sculpture simultaneously —an approach called arts integration.

McKinley K-8 School of Integrated Arts created a positive school culture through its art programs. Photo: Author.

In his novel, "Long Division," Kiese Laymon wrote, "Only those who can read, write and love can move forward and backward in time." The power of literacy also flows through music, song, dance and image making. When the arts and culture are included in the curriculum the possibilities of literacy and learning are expanded 360 degrees to include the full breadth of human communications technologies, both ancient and futuristic.

Children deserve to be welcomed into the world of knowledge. There is no reason rigorous study cannot be laced with fun. I imagine schools of the future as circular rather than hierarchical, community-nourished rather than individualistic. We can reimagine teaching and learning from art forms that have been regenerated through community process. For example, the art of Capoeira happens in a roda, or in the round. It is knit together through intergenerational relationships and performed through movement and call and response singing. Capoeiristas learn the history and geography from improvising in a ritual structure. Our bodies skim the floor and become airborne through spins and inversions, all this during healthful teaching and learning.

Children learn capoeira roda rituals with author
and Mestre Amen Santo at the Brasil Brasil Cultural Center,
(L-R: Amy, Lukaza, Amen, Kenya, Reva, and Sandra Jay)

I've come to see education as a shared endeavor — a collaborative investment to welcome the next generation into the circle and fortify them as harbingers of the future. Including the arts and culture in education allows children to know themselves and each other as culture makers — people endowed with the tremendous powers of the imagination.

During the making of the Artbound special, "Arts Education," I visited public schools throughout L.A. County with a team of documentarians. This gave me an opportunity to see how inclusive arts education builds communities where students, teachers and neighborhoods can thrive.

Murals outside Los Angeles High School of the Arts, Photo: Author

CONNECTING HOME AND SCHOOL CULTURES

At Los Angeles High School for the Arts, you can feel the impact of arts education on the school culture in every classroom — from theater to language arts, and geometry to biology. In one science classroom we visited, a line graph arced across the white board with formulas scribbled below. Handmade models of internal human organs adorned the space that students made from felt, crochet and beadwork.

This is how your body works. You, and your body, are a miraculous creative and scientific project.

Curiosity, artistry, and intellectualism combine to create a welcoming, exciting place to learn. This is what a science classroom feels like in a public high school for the arts. Students were teamed up to solve the problem on the board. I walked around the class observing the students' collaborative process and asked them about their work.

"Chemistry?" I guessed.

"Yes," a teenager said. "It's fun."

I nodded, returned his smile and asked to meet his teacher. The young man pointed across the room.

"There's Melendez." He taught me, "They is their pronoun."

I walked over and introduced myself to his teacher, Juan Melendez, a creative nerd who enjoys teaching.

"What is it like to teach science at school of the arts?" I asked.

Light streamed through the windows. I'd already observed the school's theater program earlier that day. We visited a classroom with sewing machines, costumes on mannequins, colorful sketches and architectural maquettes made by students. We'd witnessed student teams present original set and lighting designs, peeked into an acting rehearsal and walked through a recreation of the historical Coconut Grove Theater designed by esteemed African American architect Paul Revere Williams. I was impressed by the students' respectful, nonchalant comfort with collaboration throughout. Students were excelling in the performing arts, but how was this impacting their learning community across the curriculum?

"I can teach more," Melendez said. "This set of students is willing to go where I want them to go. They are resilient."

After teaching in other secondary schools, Melendez preferred teaching science to students who study the arts. Physiology lent itself to three-dimensional work, he mentioned.

I studied the detailed silver stitching on a biologically accurate model of the human heart made by a high school student.

"It's a lot about self-expression," Melendez said. "There are different ways to teach. They are learning in a creative way."

Melendez believed that students' exposure to design made them detail-oriented and confident in visualizing their ideas, while their background in theater made them open and communicative.

Down the hall, math teacher Andrés Galan wore matching fluorescent red glasses and guayabera, a lightweight men's summer shirt. Formulas and calculations were all over the walls, but we also found a drum set, guitar and microphone in his math class. At lunch, students gathered there to do homework, and perform romantic ballads on the guitar in Spanish.

Edwin Reconco, a PEN America Fellow and Language Arts teacher, said that "creativity helps writers communicate meaning." Students in his class used audio and web technologies to broadcast their stories through their podcast The Four-0-Eight. The podcast website states: "How often do some people pause to listen to us teenagers? To our stories? Our fears? Our hopes and dreams? The Four-0-Eight is our space. It's here for us to emerge with a voice that is loud, powerful and proud."

You know you are in a good place when your inner child whispers, "I wish I could have gone to school here." Rereading my notes from the site visit, I found in curly blue ink: "Kids and teachers get to be smart here."

ENTHUSIASM FOR LEARNING

One brisk morning, we visited McKinley K-8 School of Integrated Arts in a well-cared-for historical building in Compton, California. The school entryway sports images of children in colorful attire interspersed with playful polka dots. The colors, shapes and smiles signal that this is a space for kids.

"We were the school that no one knew existed," grinned the Principal Jennifer Moon.

"Everything goes hand in hand. The arts lead into everything else." (Since this writing, Moon became the Director of Educational Services at Compton Unified School District.)

We met teacher leaders charged with instructing students in all subject areas and providing the groundwork for students' education.

Tahasijan Taylor, a lead arts educator who specializes in dance, was a galvanizing force on their team. The teachers' enthusiasm was palpable.

"Learning doesn't happen the same way for everyone," Taylor said.

Teachers took positive risks to invest in student creativity, and the school became a place where children and teachers could flourish. They created a welcoming culture at school where children in the neighborhood could flourish. They wrangled mildly used art tables for students and turned an ordinary classroom into an open space for choreography and performance equipped with a dance-friendly floor and mirrors. The school serves an important purpose in the neighborhood. Many of the students struggle to have their basic needs met, including access to housing and meals, much less broadband and technology. They welcome students who are navigating the foster care system or facing homelessness.

"Our students go through a lot of trauma," one teacher said.

Principal Moon explained that the school had not always been such a positive place. Before this team of educators gained momentum, McKinley was the first school in California to be declared a "parent trigger school." Parent trigger, or parent empowerment, provisions were enacted by the California Department of Education in 2006 for "persistently lowest-achieving schools." In McKinley's case, the charter school company that intended to take over the helm was proven fraudulent, and it remained under the auspices of the school district rather than assuming an independent charter school structure.

It turns out that their arts-rich approach resulted in positive changes in attendance, behavior, literacy, and satisfaction — or what Moon called "smiles on their faces."

This elementary school chose to grow a thriving learning community through the arts. They wove the arts into goal setting and assessment procedures, included the arts in teacher professional development across all grade levels and provided weekly instruction in music, dance, and visual arts to students. The school has become a place of pride for the neighborhood, and a site for exchange between local residents and regional collaborators.

"Arts education has had a profound impact on our students — from an academic, social, and emotional perspective" states the school's annual report. "Our art programs have also helped foster a remarkable school culture and positive climate for students and community." Moon explained that they tried out new methods and evaluated their progress to guide each step forward.

"That kids come to school daily is a blessing," said Moon. "[But] they have to take tests, and they have to show growth."

It turns out that their arts-rich approach resulted in positive changes in attendance, behavior, literacy, and satisfaction — or what Moon called "smiles on their faces." The annual report reveals that "since the inception of our various art programs, attendance rates have increased 6% (from 2016 - 2019), disciplinary office referrals have decreased by 18%, and students who have met or exceeded ELA [English Language Arts] have increased by 27%." In sum, more children are showing up to learn, feeling comfortable at school, and gaining the power of literacy.

As an Angeleno born during the Watts Rebellion, whose son was born just before the L.A. Rebellion, I couldn't help but notice that this successful team was intercultural. Moon is Korean American; Taylor is African American. The children and arts teacher leaders we met were African American and Latinx. Moon grew up in L.A.'s Koreatown, and her parents lost their clothing store during the rebellion. She became the first Korean American in Administration in the Compton Unified School District (CUSD), dutifully mentored by an Assistant Superintendent who was also an immigrant, but of African origin. She has been with the district for 17 years now, and her immigrant experience grew into compassion for the struggles and aspirations of her students' families. Taylor was born and raised in South Los Angeles. She brought her depth of knowledge and commitment to children through the arts. Together they inspired a community of educators and students.

"We are learning that we are arts teachers," one teacher said. "I am art. It was a shift in our thinking."

After the meeting, we observed classes, including a dance rehearsal. Children practiced a choreography set to the song "Stand Up" by Cynthia Erivo. The children were utterly focused, determined to bring Tubman's story to light. The dancers were grouped into three tableaus, and the emotion of the music honoring Harriet Tubman's courage came through their kinesthetic expression. They moved together with slow sustained gestures, reaching and contracting to the lyrics of the song. After their performance, students fielded responses to our questions about their work. Their pride and pleasure in their performance shone through.

REIMAGINING COMMUNITY

Paulo Freire, the late Brazilian educational philosopher, defined literacy as "reading the world and reading the word." Powerful learning helps us understand what is within us, around us, and beyond what we see in our daily lives.

Our regional culture is a mosaic of identities, and, according to the last census, 27% of Californians are foreign-born. It is no wonder that California is a hub of the creative economy because the arts and culture grow from the same root. The work of artists is to make culture.

We cultivate the qualities of open-mindedness, cultural competency and empathy at the intersection of self and community. The arts provide ways to learn from history, and to refresh how we see ourselves and each other.

California is a vibrant, intercultural region. No longer can we speak of minorities and majorities when it comes to who we are. Cultural competency is everyone's homework — in school, at home and at work. When students make art, they are reimagining and remaking themselves, the culture of their schools, neighborhoods, and futures. Arts and cultural education help us do the important work of reimagining self and community. Every time a child creates, and is seen or heard, a new door to the future opens.

COMMUNITIES

Youth Arts Leadership Project. Photo: Reva Santo, Collage: Author.

"Do Our Lives Matter?": music, poetry, and Freedom School

Tara sits in the sun by a row of scrawny trees that provide no shade. She is a respected youth leader at the Community Coalition (COCO) about to begin her senior year of high school. [1] My son Avila and I have been teaching arts education at Freedom School. Earlier that week two black men— Philando Castile and Alton Sterling—were killed by police in front of their friends and families. The violent summer left a suffocating sensation in my chest that I couldn't shake off. But it was time to teach, and teaching is inherently an investment in hope (Ginwright, 2015)

"Good to see you." I walk up the steps to greet her.

We look out at the younger children who are playing ball beneath a crop of eucalyptus trees: "I'm afraid for them," she says.

I nod. Exhale. We are standing in a sun that's too hot.

"Let's talk about it in class."

We push open the heavy doors of the building to set up for class. Takara scribbles a list on the blackboard in chalk. 'Black Lives Matter', she writes. 'Black & Brown. My Life Matters. Self love'.

Teens enter the classroom, melt into rolling chairs, and circle around tables. We facilitate a group brainstorm. Tara documents students' ideas on the board. Layla, an eleventh grader, who leads her high school in basketball, bends forward and steps toward the board as if to make a dunk. She writes across the flat surface 'Do our lives matter?'

The aims of the arts education program quickly pivoted to address her question. The guiding tenet became supporting the holistic lives of youth that are too often overlooked; black and brown lives matter. We would use music and poetry to amplify the experiences and value of children's lives. Students interrogated public culture and public policy, developed multiple literacies in music and writing, and activated platforms for youth voice on personal and social issues. Teens performed their artwork for peers, families, and communities to represent themselves on their own terms, reclaim access to a local park, and help get out the vote (Mihalik et al., 2016). [2]

This essay introduces readers to the geographical, cultural, and institutional aspects of an educational project based in South Los Angeles (SLA). It is structured around methodology (key questions, conceptual framework, and participatory methods) and transformational stories. I will say, from the outset, that I view storytelling as meaningful social action. "Stories are what we have, the barometers by which we fashion our identities, organize and live our lives, connect and com- pare our lives to others, and make decisions about how to live" (Ellis, 2009: 16). Storytelling vignettes, culled from ethnography and autoethnography, draw attention to teaching and learning processes and outcomes. The first story discusses how Avila and I aimed to unleash the creative assets of novice teachers. The second story follows how we activated multiple literacies across content areas through poetry and music. The third story reveals difficult conversations about violence and uses creative writing to reimagine future possibilities. The work culminates with short-term project outcomes, and longer-term implications for change (Walker, 2018).

Avila Santo teaches music production to youth leaders. Photo: Reva Santo.

FAMILY, COMMUNITY, AND PLACE

Youth learn through the arts and culture at home, at school, and in the community. My first teachers were my family, and my children have both co-taught with me and facilitated their own teaching and learning experiences. My work is multi-disciplinary and connects the arts, education, and urban planning. Avila, my son, is a musician and composer. My daughter Reva is a multimedia storyteller. In this project, Avila taught music production, I taught poetry, and Reva served as the project's visual documentarian (Santo, 2017b). I am of Jewish origin. My ancestors fled Europe due to fascism and life threatening antisemitism. My mother's family relocated to the Middle East, and my father's came to the United States. My children's father is black and immigrated to the United States from Brazil. While my children and I were born in LA, we have immediate family ties to three continents. Our family is intercultural, interfaith (Jewish and Ifa), and polylingual (English, Spanish, and Portuguese). Being from an intercultural family has not resulted in colorblindness, as some people might expect. Instead, it has made us more adept at navigating differences. There were many moments along the way when children in this particular project questioned our identities, their own, and those of the black and brown artists whose work we studied in class. Multiplicity was central to the teaching and learning process, and echoed COCO's larger aims of black and brown solidarity.

The Freedom School project was in a burgeoning cultural capital of the United States (Los Angeles County Arts Commission, 2017; Shimshon-Santo, 2018). South Los Angeles is a hub for West Coast hip-hop music, culture, and fashion. Local creativity is world-class and deeply rooted. Local artists of color have fueled artistic and social innovation, spawned cultural spaces, and passed down knowledge through intergenerational mentorship. LA's District 8 is primarily black and Latinx—44% black and 41% speak Spanish at home (Census Bureau QuickFacts, 2018). [3]

Community arts spaces provide permeable sites for teaching, learning, and invention. While South Los Angeles is an organic conservatory of arts, culture, and entrepreneurship, it is also grossly underinvested (Jackson, 2014; Lipsitz, 2011; McKittrick and Woods, 2007). Access to arts education in schools echoes larger inequalities in social investments (CREATE CA, 2015). Living conditions in District 8 have been framed by racist and xenophobic practices and policies (including restrictive housing covenants, redlining, underinvestment in public schools, and police brutality) that are still felt today. COCO is in District 8 where residents earn the lowest wages of any district in LA. Of the local unsheltered population, 83% are black and 24% are youth (Los Angeles County Housing Authority (LAHSA), 2017).

Carlos Perez, aka "Preacher," poses with two mentees. Photo: Author.

WELCOME TO FREEDOM SCHOOL

COCO provides educational, college preparatory, and family-friendly programs activating community organizing to improve living conditions in the neighborhood. COCO manages the LA chapter of Freedom School. Freedom schools were named in 1964 during freedom summer in Mississippi, a popular education program organized by the Student Nonviolent Coordinating Committee (SNCC) to invest in black children locked into poorly resourced segregated schools. Freedom schools 'seek to build strong, literate, and empowered children prepared to make a difference in themselves, their families, communities, nation and world' (Children's Defense Fund, 2018). A national network of Freedom Schools now crisscrosses the

United States and is managed by the Children's Defense Fund (CDF) founded by Marion Wright Edelman 40 years ago.

COCO is located on the corner of Vermont Avenue near 81st Street across from a church, an empty lot, and Glady's 98 Cent Store. The Vermont corridor was a major site of burning during the civil uprising in 1992. Founded in 1989 by local activists and health care worker Karen Bass, 'Community Coalition was born as an African American and Latino organization.' The goal was 'to organize the community to turn despair and hopelessness into action' (Community Coalition, 2016). Twenty-five years later, Ms. Bass became our Congresswoman representing the 37th District of the State of California, and now serves as the city Mayor. Residents also elected Marqueece Harris-Dawson (former Executive Director of COCO) to represent District 8 on the LA City Council. COCO aims to tackle the root causes of poverty, crime, and violence through community organizing, policy change, educational and community programs, and long-term mentorship.

PROJECT EVOLUTION

The prior summer, Avila and I were invited to read aloud and perform at Freedom School, and this ignited the desire for more. How might we incorporate arts education into the Freedom School curriculum emphasizing literacy, college preparation, and political education? During the project planning phase, Avila asked, 'what would school be like if everyone learned how to read music and play music like they learned how to read and write?'

It is important for youth to see themselves as creators, not just consumers, of culture. 'I want to show [students] that ... music doesn't come from YouTube', Avila said. 'Music doesn't come from SoundCloud. Music comes from *you*. And it comes from your surroundings and from people and from sounds ...' (Santo, 2017a).

Avila and I discussed how teaching could support the pursuit of freedom. 'How can we as oppressed people reach liberation through the words of our oppression?' he asked:

"What do you mean by the words of our oppression?" I ask. "What's an example?"

"English," he says.

He said the word English like it was a wall, a hard surface without a door to enter.

"Certain things don't translate because it's not in the consciousness of English."

Is English a container or a consciousness? Maybe both.

"So, is music another language for you?" I ask.

"Absolutely."

We chose to define literacy as communications and positioned music on an equal plane with the written word.

Our family conversations led to planning meetings with the Executive Vice-President Aurea Montes-Rodriguez, and Freedom School Director Melanie Kimes, to co-define shared aims. Our goal was to provide a culturally rich arts education, rooted in black and brown creativities, that facilitated opportunities for youth to grow as leaders through music production and creative writing. Winning a small grant from the Department of Cultural Affairs (DCA) allowed us to offer arts education classes at Freedom School all summer long the following year.

METHODOLOGY

The key questions guiding this project were: How can arts education affirm the lives of Freedom School students and teachers? How can music and poetry cultivate multiple literacies and local knowledge? How can arts education accelerate political awareness and leadership development? This section overviews key theoretical debates and introduces the participatory ethos behind our method, or approach to inquiry and action.

Creativity is a powerful current for teaching, learning, and social change. W.E.B. Du Bois (1926) believed that the arts are important to liberation. For him, the arts ask critical questions like: 'What do we want? What is the thing we are after?' Creative expression can unlock the power of self-determination, and help people imagine what is not currently possible (Bell, 2005; Du Bois, 1926; Hill-Collins, 2008). There are myriad examples of artistic practices linked to community organizing—consider capoeira, the blues, and black civil rights; teatro, muralism, and the Chicano movement; spoken word, poetry, and intersectional feminism, to name a few (Anzaldúa, 1987; Broyles-González, 1994; Do Nascimento, 1987; Lorde, 1984; Woods, 1998). Artists and writers committed to social justice have interrogated how culture and identity are hinged to political and economic liberation, and how storytelling and story listening can inform ethical leadership and human rights efforts (Césaire, 2017; James, 1963; Maeda, 2014; Moore, 2009). Ella Baker rejected a charismatic leadership approach in favor of broad-based youth development through grassroots organizing (Ransby, 2003). Her approach influenced Marion Wright Edelman and the Freedom Schools. This project presents arts education as a strategy for political consciousness raising and leadership development.

Paulo Freire (1970) envisioned a teaching practice that recognizes students' lives and what they know. In this case, we used poetry and music production to express different realities and co-create. Employing arts integration techniques, we juxtaposed content areas, cultural contexts, and learning modalities associated with self-efficacy, and literacy acquisition (Gardner, 1983; Greenfader et al., 2015; Shimshon-Santo, 2010b, 2017; Hanley and Noblit, 2009; Weiss, 2008).

"The processes of research," Askins (2011) writes, "are as important as the empirical and knowledge outcomes and are inseparable from them" (p. 807). Simply put, how one goes about doing things shapes what one comes to know and the outcomes of one's knowledge and action. The essay is informed by two processes of inquiry: (1) participatory action research (PAR), and 2) autoethnography. The objective of PAR is to 'investigate reality in order to transform it' (Askins, 2011; Fals Borda, 2006: 353, 2013). Over time, the arts have become accepted as a viable PAR strategy 'for participant self-representation within a framework of coproduction of knowledge for social justice' (Askins, 2011). Autoethnography is a method where the researcher openly positions her voice within the social inquiry. Ellis (2009) describes the auto ethnographer as 'the person at the intersection of the personal and the cultural, thinking and observing as an ethnographer and writing and describing as a storyteller' (p. 13). The auto ethnographer conveys meaning, transmits creative tensions, and provides insights via thoughtful writing and storytelling. Together, the participatory ethos imbued in both methods—PAR and autoethnography—fit my intention of including myself, my family, and the community in the process of co-determining shared aims, procedures, and desired outputs.

Many LA residents belong to more than one culture, language, faith, or nationality. Cultural relevance requires educators to be attentive to intersectionality (Anzaldúa, 1987; Crenshaw, 1991; Lorde, 1984). Cultural multiplicity has deep roots in the region. The first *pobladores* of Los Angeles, after the indigenous Tongva nation, were an intercultural group of indigenous, black, and European origins, the majority of which were of mixed ancestry (Mason, 2004). However, racist and sexist ideas, practices, and policies have institutionalized hierarchies that privilege white- ness (Lipsitz, 2016; Lorde, 1984; Morrison, 1990). In this project, we prioritized music and literature of the black and Latinx diasporas. Eurocentrism and androcentrism are undergirded by epistemic racism and sexism. Epistemic racism exists alongside white supremacist and misogynist physical violence. The term epistemicide is a mash up of epistemology (the theory of knowledge, or what one believes is true) and genocide (the deliberate killing of large groups of people) (De Sousa Santos, 2014). This term conveys the gravity of what is at stake: identities, knowledge, and lives. I view artistic expression as a decolonizing practice where one can rehearse the habits of thinking and feeling for oneself while practicing social critique, developing empathy, and imagining alternative possibilities (Catterall, 2009; Catterall et al., 2012; Dabashi, 2015; Mignolo, 2015).

Technological changes have also disrupted simplistic notions of literacy, and how people organize for social change (Fantin, 2011; Lucas, 2012; Tufekci and Talbot, 2016). I use social media as both a pedagogical strategy and an action research technique to (1) amplify and affirm youth voice and (2) gauge my own accuracy by hearing how participants and their followers react to messaging. I remember hearing Jay-Z's mom on *The Black Album* say she gave her son a boom box to keep him out of trouble (Carter, 2003). I use the technologies of our time. My generation was the boombox. Avila's generation was sampling, mixed tapes on CD, and mp4s, software like Scratch, Reason, Serato, and Ableton. We now toggle between analogue, digital, and web platforms in our teaching and creative practices. Home, school, and community (both landed and virtual) are spaces for teaching and learning, research, and action (Young, 1997). For transnational and intercultural families, it is particularly important to facilitate multiple, culturally rich, spaces. Connecting home, school, and community can disrupt the boundaries between home and school cultures, the fabricated private and public spheres, and limited national imaginaries (Anzaldúa, 1987; Ortner, 1974).

Student performs his composition in class. Photo: Reva Santo.

UNLEASHING CREATIVE CONFIDENCE

An energetic group of novice teachers gather in a room beneath an enormous aquamarine portrait of Trayvon Martin, the black teen whose slaying in Florida in 2013 by a white vigilante sparked the Black Lives Matter movement. When you look closely, Martin's portrait is made of myriad tiny faces of people in the community. Our goal was to affirm teachers' creative and cultural assets and provide strategies for them to incorporate the arts in the classroom. We also expanded their definitions of literacy to include multiple modes of communication (Fantin, 2011; Lucas, 2012).

Avila and I introduce ourselves through our creative habits and ask everyone to do the same:

"My name is Avila. I'm a musician and composer."

"I'm Amy. I grew up in dance and am now a writer and poet."

The teachers mention cooking, singing, poetry, spoken word, drama, and surfing music on SoundCloud. Teachers map a brainstorm on the wall of their shared creative assets. Our strategy is to teach an art class while modeling how to teach an art class, so we guide the activities and explain each step. We ask: how are music and writing similar or different, and what tools do musicians and writers use to compose? Our academic terms are composition, sampling, looping, quoting, and repetition. We introduce the arts education strands for lesson planning and draw connections between music and language literacy (SAEDAE, 2014). Sampling in music is like quoting in writing; looping in music is like repetition in writing. Students will be able to recognize a loop in music and use repetition in their writing.

Avila stands at his computer with a projection of his interface on the wall behind him. He is a musical astronaut facing a sonic console. We travel with him to hear sound samples from George Clinton and Parliament, Igor Stravinsky, and Max Roach. George Clinton is a black artist born in the United States and a pioneer of funk and rock music in the 1970s and 1980s. His signature mash-up sound and early sampling with P-Funk, Parliament, and Funkadelic were foundational for hip-hop. Igor Stravinsky was a white pianist and conductor raised in Russia during the 1900s. Max Roach grew up in North Carolina in the 1940s and was a black jazz and bebop music pioneer and drummer. They each reached global audiences. By placing Clinton, Stravinsky, and Roach together, Avila demarcates an inclusive sonic historical geography on his own terms.

I introduce three writers: Terrance Hayes (born in South Carolina in 1971), Sandra Cisneros (born in Chicago in 1954), and Sonia Sanchez (born in Alabama in 1934) whose approach to rhythm, improvisation, and spoken word was influenced by performing with jazz musician Max Roach. I chose a public health epidemic relevant to COCO's history as a writing prompt. Addiction is the focus of a poem we listen to by Terrance Hayes (2015) called "Lighthead's Guide to Addiction."

The teachers generate lists of addictions and their alternatives, select their favorite, and perform them together. The microphone summons an invisible spotlight. Avila records their shared performance poem. Each line is written by a different teacher, and sequenced using chance composition based on their place in the circle:

If you are addicted to music / Try silence
If you are addicted to attention / Try stepping back
If you are addicted to working / Try relaxing
If you are addicted to commitment / Try running
If you are addicted to defending / Try walking away
If you are addicted to complaining / Try listening
If you are addicted to profanity / Try being a nun
If you are addicted to silence / Try thunderous
If you are addicted to hate / Try empathy
If you are addicted to money/ Try credit
If you are addicted to speaking / Try apologizing—just once
If you are addicted to finding love / Try loving yourself
If you are addicted to thugging it out / Try crying
If you are addicted to gated communities / Try Section 8
If you are addicted to texting / Try disposable thumbs
If you are addicted to hurting yourself / Try me

The room feels electrified by the power of their voices. The session recuperates connections between language and music often severed in classrooms while affirming cultural assets and bolstering teachers' curiosity and creative confidence.

Avila Santo teaches beat making with youth. Photo: Author.

FOUND POETRY AND BEAT MAKING

There is a small circle of stones on the floor, a miniature Stonehenge on gray carpet. Avila claims the teacher's desk with his computer, microphone, keyboard, and LaunchPad. A Launchpad is an electronic grid instrument used with Ableton Live that permits triggering digital sounds to create spontaneous compositions. I open the blinds to let in light and stand before the chalkboard. The students arrive with backpacks and chatter. No one disturbs the tiny circle of painted rocks on the floor. It's an unspoken oddity no one budges or discusses. We look at it. Hop over it. Leave it where it is.

Avila and I introduce our goals to make found poems and compose music from found sounds. Found poetry is 'the literary equivalent of a collage ... often made from newspaper articles, street signs, graffiti, speeches, letters, or even other poems' (Academy of American Poets, 2017). In 'One Boy Told Me', Naomi Shihab-Nye (2009) sequenced things her son said during his first two years of life.

The poem highlights a child's imagination and questioning—important things like 'can noodles swim?' and 'what does minus mean? / I never want to minus you'.

We recite Shihab-Nye's found poem aloud in popcorn style, each student reading one line at a time to establish a ritual of speaking and listening. I ask students to note their favorite lines and share their favorite parts. Students like what the boy says about music living inside his body, so I write that on the board: 'Music lives inside my legs.'

"Start with this line and add on your own," I suggest.

Pens and pencils flow across sheets of paper. We collect their favorite lines into group poems. Here is one: 'music lives in my legs / I hear it in my head / it echoes through the halls / to a door I haven't seen / it whispers behind me, again and again / music is important to me'. A tween wearing a Legends Never Die t-shirt wants to read it aloud. *We did that*, you can see in his eyes. A bit of magic. Everyone looks pleased. We are now officially poets.

When it is time for music, a bunch of students jump up out of their seats. A student who struggled during the reading section is thrilled with the prospect of making his own sounds. He trans- forms from the shy one in the corner during writing to the brave one leading the show in music. I notice. Avila notices. Everyone notices. He is letting everyone see this important aspect of his personality and brilliance.

Students swarm around Avila like bees in their own sonic hive. Accumulating one sound at a time, they build a layered track using a microphone, keyboard, and Launch Pad. Faces grin as new sounds are invented in the moment. They are making music. Something powerful is going on. They slow down the collage of beats and vocals into a haunting spooky soundscape. *It echoes*, the loop chants, *it echoes*.

LOVE IS A NOT A GUN

Helena calls me over before class. She has long dark hair, black-rimmed glasses, and a neon phone case. Her mother is on COCO's parent leadership committee, and her family is originally from Central America: "I found something," she says. "Listen to this."

She shows me a book about Emmett Till and places her phone on the table to play me a song. Emmett Till was born in Mississippi in 1941. He was a black child, murdered by a white mob in 1955. The book begins with Till as a hopeful child and closes with images of his face, swollen like a ghostly melon after being beaten and lynched by white racists.

"See what they did to him?" she says.

"Yes."

My heart explodes. I mold my face into a neutral expression and prepare to discuss what's on her mind. She selects a song and sound emerges from the device. The lyrics scroll across the small screen in bold red type. Heavy metal: "Love is like handing someone a gun," she repeats from the lyrics. "Your arms are open. They can shoot!" *More heartbreak.* "Have you felt that before?" I ask.

"No," she says. She looks calm about the whole thing. She could have been talking about bunny rabbits or sneakers.

Oh. I get it. She's studying. It's some life lesson kind of thing. "I'm not sure if I agree with that metaphor," I say. We had studied metaphors last class. "Does love have to be a gun?"

Her attention turns to the book.

"He was 14," she says.

She is 14, too. We flip through the pages together. She points to the image of a child in a casket—his mouth a tiny nib on his bludgeoned gray moon face:

"The police did that to him," she says.

"Yes," I say. "They did."

My body is a mountain seated before her, still as rock. *Children shouldn't be in danger. Children should not be murdered.* I'm a volcano inside. Furious at a world that permits such atrocities. We wobble quietly in our webbed plastic chairs. *Does love have to be a gun? Why are love and lynching in the same frame?*

"If you love someone who loves you back," I say, "it might not be like a gun."

She unplugs the phone from its charger and spins it in a circle on the linoleum table like a game of Russian roulette. I don't want to lie. The truth is, I was thinking about a gun just last night. Early that morning, around 3:00 am, I felt the tip of a cold metal pushing against my temple. I was stand- ing there behind myself—one woman lying down, one woman standing up. I'd come to kidnap myself, to lead myself away from danger. It was an act of self-defense. Lucid dreaming.

"If you could see through me / Si pudieses ver dentro de mi" poster.

"Our Voice. Our Vote." poster featuring Ryan Bell.
Photos: Reva Santo; Poster Designs: Anthony Phills.

"If you love someone else," I say, "it doesn't mean they have complete control over you ... Just last night, I used a gun to kidnap myself back."

She doesn't blink an eye, or look at me like I'm crazy, or question if it was a real or symbolic gun. Sometimes a metaphor comes in handy. Sometimes a metaphor is, in fact, a gun. She seems pleased with the advice. In less than 24 hours my own struggle had become useful to another soul.

"You can choose a different metaphor," I say. "You can choose something else."

LET'S BUILD A WHOLE NEW NATION

Alfred holds a bouquet of colorful balloons tethered together by curly ribbons. He is a lighthouse for families to find the culminating performance at Freedom School. A teacher named Ryan leads the crowd of students, teachers, parents, and grandparents in Harambee chants that shake the walls, ricocheting joy everywhere. Teachers receive awards from the State of California for their service to children, and students present speeches, skits, and compositions.

Mia and Tara introduce our team of young artists.

"Welcome," Mia says. "In music production, we learned how to create music through samples, midi instruments, and live triggering on a Launchpad. We also learned how to listen to music by doing field recordings, song instrumentation, and basic arrangement." She passes the mic to Tara.

"In creative writing class, we read poets like Lucille Clifton, Terrance Hayes, and Maya Angelou, and rappers including Public Enemy and KRS- One. We wrote our own work and practiced public speaking that is important for leaders to know."

It was an election year and COCO had been organizing to get out the vote. While children can't vote, they can raise awareness of propositions and candidates.

"103 million people in the United States are unable to voice their opinions," Jacqueline says drawing from voting rights data we studied in poetry class.

Tara recites "Ineligibility," a poem posted on our process blog and SoundCloud page (Haslem, 2016).

Ineligibility / That's there I stand / But I'm not alone / About 103 million people in the / U.S. stand where I stand / The homeless / The felons / The children / The undocumented / Stand with me / While we stand together / We watch as the eligible / make the decisions for us / We watch / As the eligible make change / For better or for worse / We shall not say a word because it would not be heard / For we are the ineligibles / That stand together / But alone.

The students join her on stage, grab hands, and bow as an ensemble. Boisterous applause.

A few weeks later, the youth are invited to perform at COCO's Power Fest in Martin Luther King Park to help reclaim safe public spaces for recreation in the neighborhood. This project affirmed the cultures, imaginations, and possibilities of students and teachers and complemented COCO's broader community organizing goals for voter participation, public health, and intergenerational connection. It affirmed a precedent for including arts education in Freedom School moving forward and gave COCO one more way to include the arts in their mission driven work.

Wind whips through the car windows as Avila and I drive home.

"I remember what it feels like to be unheard in a classroom," he says. Long silence. He taps a persistent beat on the floor with his foot and plays a polyrhythm on his shoulder with his opposite hand. In other words, he is thinking. Tangerine light illuminates the windshield. "What they did was completely state of the art. People had nothing but good things to say."

I squint and smile. Avila has become the solution to the problems he faced in school as a child. My child has grown up to make the childhood of other children a little better.

Months later, I meet up with Tara and Jaqueline at a COCO event celebrating the 25th Anniversary of the LA uprising (McGahan, 2017). These young women look more grown: a nose ring, a slightly taller stance, eagerness. They tell me about the colleges they've been accepted to. Jacqueline's broad grin activates the fist-muscle inside my chest. This is no mountaintop, but it might as well be. A family. A community. A city. I can hear life's rhythm regenerating.

Manuela García and friends, 1901. Photo: Charles Lummis.
Courtesy Autry Museum Archive.

Born in Los Angeles on Los Angeles Street

Manuela García's devotion to music amplifies the feminine voice in the sonic history of the Southwest. Over 100 wax cylinders of her singing were carefully preserved in the Autry Museum's archive, but her story had been separated from her songs. In one sepia photograph, she gazes out of frame. In another, she stands with a group of women by the trunk of a thick-limbed tree, branches wide as elephant legs. I was asked to write a poem to honor her for the centennial of women's suffrage. To celebrate her in poetry we first had to restore the missing link between inert archival objects and her life.

I first learned of Manuela García from curator Janice Ngan at a Korean restaurant on Olympic Boulevard over bowls of spicy tofu stew. Ngan wanted to highlight García's wax recordings at a public engagement event for the exhibition *What's Her Story*. As we savored pickled cabbage and scraped the stone bottom of a bowl of bibimbap, Janice's imagination levitated between us above the savory plates. I saw people walking through shafts of sound beamed across the museum courtyard like Star Trek teleportation. These wax recordings are recognized at the root of Latinx music in L.A., but our hemispheric research revealed that they are also the earliest known recordings of classic Mexican songs anywhere in the Americas.

The pandemic reached California shortly after Ngan introduced me to community engagement producer Brittany Campbell, and music producer John Hendicott. We pivoted to the live event to broadcast online and adhere to public health mandates. I reached out to Ani Boyadjian who enlisted a team of special collections librarians from the Los Angeles Public Library (LAPL) to unearth information on García's life including her studies, professions, dwellings, and family members. The librarians introduced us to Marissa Lopez who was excited to map García's history in space.

As a writer, I wanted to see García's pages. She curated her ideas in her diary. Music and handwriting were her personal technologies. On the cover of her journal, she wrote: "— 1901 —, Manuela García, 1115 S. Olive St., Los Angeles." With the museum facility shuttered, and her last recorded dwelling now a parking lot, we even toyed with the idea of projecting her sounds and images on the walls of downtown skyscrapers. Eventually, we chose cyberspace.

García crowned the first page of her notebook with the number one, drawn with a sharp angled hat. Beneath the number was a song written in impeccable cursive lettering on an unlined page. She drew a mark through the first word in the title, "Besos," and floated the corrected spelling "Versos" above it. Kisses and verses. Her editorial mark inspired the name of the project: *Versos y Besos: The Anthrophony of Manuela García.*

At first, I misread her handwriting "Versos del Alba" (Verses of the Dawn) as "Versos de Luta" (Verses of Mourning). This reflected my mindset during quarantine. Daniel Bellm corrected mourning to dawn (luta to alba), and blood to willow (sang to sauz) in the line: "el sauz y la palma se mecen con calma." García's message to us during a pandemic (inside a 100-year-old journal-bottle) was to find calm, recognize beauty, and value companionship.

I'm no mariachi, but I think like a capoeirista. The art of capoeira survived tremendous odds due to cultural practitioners' dedication to education and performance. I reached out to mariachi Jasmín Morales to see if she recognized García's repertoire and sent the songs to Delia Xóchitl Chávez from the Mexican Secretary of Culture. The song on the first page of García's diary had become a mariachi standard sung throughout the region. Chavez traced the path of the song through publication histories. The song had been copy written by a male artist in Mexico fifty years after it first appeared in García's diary in Los Angeles.

We could not have fulfilled this project without taking a collaborative, hemispheric approach. Working hemispherically meant being attentive to migration and culture, colonization and sovereignty. The earth is an orbiting sphere, and species migration is a natural occurrence. I am a part of those nomadic flows, and so was the family of Manuela García. California is a part of a connected landmass that faces the Pacific Ocean. 100 years later, half of L.A. residents still have familial ties to Mexico, Central and South America.

Manuela García's story illuminates the circulation of music, culture, and family between California and Mexico. The daughter of Rosario Diez and Ignacio García, she dedicated herself to study, teaching, and music. She was one of ten children born to her twice married mother. She earned a degree in business, became a teacher, studied theater, scored presentations, and threw birthday parties that made the local news. She defended her self-worth and expertise with dignity in sophisticated correspondences with Anglo male power brokers of her time. Manuela García earned her place as a respected voice of early Los Angeles, known for her cultivated knowledge of Mexican music, education, and performance.

Above: Elisa Quiñonez of Las Colibri rehearsing at La Fonda. Below: Stacy Lopez on guitarrón. Mariachi regalia on display at La Fonda, Photos: Author.

The L.A. based women's mariachi ensemble, Las Colibri, agreed to interpret the song on the first page of her diary. Suzanne García, the company director, arranged a performance of "Versos Del Alba" at La Fonda—an iconic local space for mariachi artists over the past fifty years. She flicked on the lights to reveal towering, embroidered mariachi regalia framed on the walls. A century after García wrote in her diary, Angelenos were still singing her song. Finally, I could write the poem.

Born in Los Angeles on Los Angeles Street

—*after Manuela C. García*

born in los angeles
by los angeles street
y la calle de negros

manuela garcía sang
of willows and palm leaves
painted blue by the sea

hija y maestra, daughter
teacher, encantadora de mundos
california-americanas

desde sinaloa hasta la porciúncula
mazatlán to the zanja madre
her worlds still strum the city's center

> coro: —
> *we read your butterfly cursive*
> *hear your cien canciones*
> *que hermosa eres tú!*
> *how beautiful you are!*

cien por ciento angelina, one
of ten children, familia hecha de música
encyclopedic manos y mentes musicales

legacies of sound, collected
dentro del cuerpo, body of metaphor
metáforas escrito a lápiz

alfabetizadíssima, the singer carried
the culture forward as student
bookkeeper, teacher, teacher of spanish

conjuring hyacinth and fern
down los angeles street, spring, olive
inhabiting six homes in seven decades

her voice skips across centuries
floating above the andes, bailando
la zamacueca in a jipijapa hat

    coro: —

    we read your butterfly cursive
    hear your cien canciones
    que hermosa eres tú!
    how beautiful you are!

la voz de manuela garcía, one woman
more than an artifact, canister of cara negra
more than a check for 12 cents a song

her life, handwritten
at the spark of women's suffrage
la chispa de un siglo feminino

mujer, no dividida
whole — before and after a treaty, la frontera
inventada crossing calles, casas, familias

her sound circulates el espacio, expansive
sonic territory, territorio abierto de pasado-futuros
songs that continue to be sung

coro: —   *continúa*

coro: —   *continúa*

coro: —   *continúa*

Participants in community conversation gather by Ofelia Esparza's altar for Dia de los Muertos at Self Help Graphics. (Left to right) Front line: Jilly Canizares, Miranda Ynez, Alexa Kim, Brittany Fields, Alma Catalan, Yolanda Hester. Back line: Amy Shimshon-Santo, Betty Avila, Francis Cullado, Joel Garcia, Kimberley Osorio, Avila Santo, Lucy Lu, Ben Caldwell, Kim Harris. Photo: Reva Santo

How to Become Erasure Proof

"If we possess the land," cultural guardian Ben Caldwell said, "we can become erasure proof." On the street, displacement from gentrification feels like banishment — or forced exile from the city. This work amplifies resilience strategies of adaptation, connection, and care by BIPOC (Black, Indigenous, People of Color) communities seeking cultural and spatial sovereignty. The axis of the essay is an intergenerational conversation with cultural producers at Self Help Graphics & Art (SHG) in the Latinx neighborhood of Boyle Heights, Kaos Network (Kaos) the African American neighborhood of Leimert Park, and Visual Communications (VC) in the Asian Pacific Islander led neighborhood of Little Tokyo. The setting for the conversation is Los Angeles — a megalopolis on the Pacific Rim recognized globally for its cultural production.

The community conversation was structured around themes of land, story, memory, and leadership. The project reveals ways BIPOC community arts spaces fortify ecologies of culture and place with local and diasporic dimensions. This paper provides information on the action research process, its themes and participants, and a conceptual framework called rethinking culture and place, before turning to ethnographic analysis of the focus group. Cultural activists catalyzed social benefits by cultivating local and diasporic creativity, expanding platforms for individual and community representation, and facilitating lifelong learning opportunities tethered to enduring relationships. In addition, by advocating with BIPOC artists, households, and neighborhoods among broader political, economic, cultural, and environmental power brokers, BIPOC arts and cultural spaces are often voices for equity and fairness in decision making regarding regional development.

PROCESS

The central concern of this inquiry was how long-standing, BIPOC community-based arts spaces have practiced spatial and cultural resilience in relation to land, story, memory, and leadership. The paper brings readers into an intergenerational, intercultural, intra-city focus group with participants from three long-standing BIPOC arts and cultural spaces in Los Angeles. The structured focus group catalyzed information sharing that could be mutually beneficial to participants while also culling qualitative data on resilience.

The focus group was one element in a larger action research process that I facilitated with community arts leaders and graduate students in arts management. The project focus responded to the desire of Miranda Ynez (a student at the time) to address the heated struggle over gentrification in her home base of East Los Angeles during her studies. Ynez hails from a family of esteemed Chicanx public artists. As an artist and educator, I've been involved with community-based arts practices for over 30 years. The process was fortified by enduring local relationships that existed prior to the focus group and that continue long after project completion. Participants were the initial editorial committee that reviewed this essay before publication.

Students and I came to refer to the project as Erasure Proof. This title was inspired by Brittany Field's fieldnotes citing Caldwell during a visit to Kaos. The project connected BIPOC graduate students and faculty with long-standing BIPOC community arts spaces in existence from 35 to 50 years. Each site was also in neighborhoods experiencing gentrification. While differing in genre and context, each site shared a commitment to BIPOC led stewardship of land and culture, racial equity, and spatial justice. The project brought the classroom closer to the city, immersed students in the important work being done by three esteemed BIPOC community arts organizations, and fortified thought partnerships among community leaders on the ground where communities were facing gentrification.

Preliminary, open-ended planning sessions with the Self Help Graphics and Art (SHG) team inspired the four themes for inquiry: land, story, memory, and leadership. I then engaged students by offering a graduate level arts management course in action research that fulfilled a capstone requirement. Each site invited participants they believed could benefit from participation in the site visits or focus group. The project mobilized a team of BIPOC arts managers completing their graduate studies: Miranda Ynez of Boyle Heights, Kimberley Osorio of South Los Angeles, Brittany Fields of Atlanta, and Lucy Lu of Beijing. Each student chose a theme that appealed most to them. Ynez chose story. Osorio studied land. Fields selected memory. Lu chose leadership. Over seven months (May through December), we spent time with the cultural sites while students studied their chosen topics. The project culminated with the focus group analyzed in this essay, and public presentations by students.

Community arts collaborators included Betty Avila, Joel Garcia, and Alexa Kim of Self Help Graphics and Art (SHG); Ben Caldwell and Kim Harris of Kaos Network (Kaos); and Francis Cullado of Visual Communications (VC). During the focus group, we also welcomed Alma Catalan (a Boyle Heights arts activist who went on to complete graduate studies in arts management); Jilly Canizares of Policy Link and former director of the Association for the Advancement of Filipino American Arts and Cultures (FilAm Arts); and Yolanda Hester, an oral historian specializing in Black entrepreneurship. Sound engineer Avila Santo, and filmmaker Reva Santo, served as documentarians for the encounter.

Fields, Osorio, and Ynez help adorn the SHG space with paper cempasúchil, representing a floral path between the present and the ancestral. Photo: Reva Santo

REORIENTING CULTURE AND PLACE

I have come to see BIPOC community art spaces as sites that generate robust ecologies of culture and place, and serve as regional anchors for community creativity, learning, and empowerment. One shared quality is their focus on cherishing culture and place (Keller et al. 2017).

Cherishing culture and place is the foundation for cultural sovereignty and community self-determination (Singel 2006). Cultural sovereignty is gained by representing "histories and existence using their own terms, and it acknowledges...self-determination as shaped by each tribe's culture, history, territory, traditions, and practices (Singel, 358: 2006). Cultural sovereignty is a counter hegemonic force against dispossession caused by settler colonialism, racism, patriarchy, and xenophobia. Dispossession, or denying people access to land or resources, disenfranchises vulnerable communities by reproducing hegemonic dominance and hierarchy (Nichols 2020). In contrast, spaces of cultural sovereignty have a cherishing effect on culture and place.

It is a valuable exercise to distinguish the qualities of culturally sovereign arts spaces. Social justice inspired art spaces often locate their origins in social movements, and their missions and ways of working differ from spaces associated with art washing (Grodach 2016; Loukaitou-Sideris 2016; Cuniffe 2016). For example, the *Protecting Ibasho* study of Little Tokyo found that "arts and culture do not automatically drive gentrification and can help slow or even stop it (Crisman 2019)." Unlike art spaces of dispossession or gentrification, culturally sovereign arts spaces fortify ecologies of culture and space that can have a protective quality on community life.

In her analysis of the U.S. caste system, Isabel Wilkerson (2020) defined eight structural pillars reinforcing social hierarchy. Among them are endogamy (relevant to family structure, housing, schooling, and segregation), terror (from individuals and the police state), and occupational hierarchy (relevant here for its impact on work life, education, and careers). The caste system reinforces false notions of superiority and inferiority (based on class, race, ethnicity, gender, faith, nativity, sexuality, educational access, etcetera), and institutes spatial policies that have a negative impact on BIPOC households and communities. Examples of this dynamic in the United States include broken treaties, restrictive housing covenants, redlining, and xenophobic displacement decrees such as Executive Order 9066.

Simply put, race is "produced by place" (Lipsitz, 5). Gilmore (2007) explains spatial racism as "the exploitation of group differentiated vulnerabilities..." 28). Pulido (2018) argues that systemic racism "is maintained by indifference" (121). Enduring equitable change requires anti-racist policy (Kendi 2019). Arguably, "policy" can exist at various scales — whether policy defined by the state, a neighborhood council, an organization, or a household.

Whether, Wilkerson's (2020) eight pillars of caste hierarchy, Lipsitz's (2011) critique of the devastating effects of overinvestment in whiteness (2011), or Kendi's (2019) demand for overly anti-racist policy, abolishing white supremacy will require liberatory material and symbolic action. The arts and culture play a role in comprehensive efforts to improve BIPOC lives — along with comprehensive broad based equity endeavors from housing to education, public health to restorative justice, and from climate change to immigration policy.

Crenshaw et al. (2019) argue that colorblindedness, or the unwillingness to see race, reproduces systems that privilege whiteness. A recent policy example of this was Proposition 209 (State of California, 1996) that employed colorblinded rhetoric to limit the ability to monitor and address obstacles to equity. California arts policy adapted to Proposition 209 in ways that reduced investments and attention to the authority of BIPOC arts and cultural spaces (Shimshon-Santo, 2003). Approximately 20 years later, Los Angeles County catalyzed an effort for arts organizations to state their commitment to diversity, equity, and inclusion (DEI).

Achieving equity will require tangible shifts in power, authority, resources, and investments that disrupt the continuity of white supremacy and systemic disenfranchisement of BIPOC communities. Lipsitz notes the "unearned advantages that whites possess" (Lipsitz 2011: 25). He wrote:

> A large and unrefuted body of research reveals how the economic standing of millions of white families today stems directly from the unfair gain and unjust enrichments made possible by past and present forms of racial discrimination. (Lipsitz 2011: 2)

It is critical to view the complex relationships between culture, place, and economics. De Lara writes that "capitalism has been enshrined as a racial project" (2018: 11). Xenophobic migration narratives are the invention of the white spatial imaginary. De Lara sees capitalist development as the "territorialization of race."

Debates about the arts and gentrification have sometimes emphasized symptoms rather than causes. When does so-called development trigger displacement? Pete White (Founder of the LA Community Action Network, CAN) clarified that "you know it's gentrification when it's not for you." Discourse on the topic has framed artists as inherently complicit with gentrification (Deutsche 1998), key stakeholders in placemaking (Jackson 2018), or as place keepers (Bedoya 2013). Research has critiqued the notion that cultural development necessarily results in displacement (Grodach 2016; Collins 2016). A study of the impact of the arts and culture on L.A.'s Little Tokyo found that arts participation provided social benefits to identity, civic engagement, and Asian Pacific Islander micro-businesses and institutions (Crisman 2019).

A variety of factors influence gentrification, including regional infrastructural development. A statewide study on gentrification revealed high rates of displacement in South California adjacent new rail hubs (Zuk et al. 2017). The study recommended protective ordinances be deployed to prevent the dispossession of low-income households and small businesses due to land speculation near new rail stops. Notably, the art spaces in this study reported gentrification near new rail stops adjacent to their sites. New rail stops were built across the street from SHG, a half block away from Kaos Network, and a block away from Visual Communications. Inadequate protective ordinances were in place. This resulted in skyrocketing commercial and residential rents which displaced cultural microbusinesses and limited the supply of affordable housing.

Community arts spaces are sites for storytelling about cultural and geographic change. Whatever the medium, storytelling is the core of an artist's work. Fuentes (1986) saw storytelling as inherently tied to power and place. The novelist wrote:

> The ancient city and that of the modern city...mirror without background for the reappearance of the other...we should not separate what we are able to imagine from what we are able to remember (Fuentes, (1986, 333).

Reclaiming time is one way of interrogating the history of racist stupidity (Onli and Johnson 2019). Onli asks "What power is worth holding? What time is worth reclaiming?" (2019 : 306) Storytelling about place makes power and time tangible.

Poet and urbanist June Jordan recognized the power of story. She wrote about spatial awareness as unfolding from the personal to the social: "you begin with your family and the kids on the block, and next you open your eyes to what you call your people and that leads you to land reform..." (2017, 2). Jordan's vision connected culture and place to the act of cherishing life.

> [S]pace cherishing...amplifies the experience of being alive, the capability of endless beginnings, and the entrusted liberty of motion; of particular space that is open-receptive communication yet sheltering particular life" (2017, 66).

Mia Birdsong (2020), advocate for families and communities, writes that the notion of belonging in the United States is wracked by contradictions.

> The Founding Fathers wrote powerfully about freedom and self-governance while inhabiting stolen land, enslaving people, and excluding most of the population from participating in that self governance (Song 2020:1).

Audre Lorde titled her first book of poetry *First Cities*, and a second *From a Land Where Other People Live*. Creating art about silenced experiences pushes society to reimagine culture and place. Lorde wrote:

> To survive in the mouth of this dragon we call America, we have had to learn this first and most vital lesson — that we were never meant to survive. Not as human beings...I speak these words as an attempt to break that silence and bridge some of those differences between us, for it is not difference which immobilizes us, but silence. And there are so many silences to be broken (1984: 41-44).

Currently, one third of Angelenos were foreign born. As a global city, L.A. is a palimpsest of the past and present, where diasporic cultures coexist in our own bodies, households, and neighborhoods. Gloria Anzaldua's (1999) creative work activated her multiple languages and connections to culture and place for Aztlán (1969). Creative expression offers potential outlets for truth telling about our lives and communities. Philanthropist Karina DeBerry argued that Black arts are an excellent barometer for understanding quality of community life. She stated,

> The reality is that the arts and culture are an economic driver for that community. It is both voice and this through line of how you can tell if a community is actually thriving. (Black Art for Thriving Communities, 2020).

Creative expression and artistic imagination can wield what Da Silva (2020) calls "the task of critique" and "the call for justice."

Author Toni Morrison (2019: 71) wrote: "My memory is as necessary to yours as yours is to mine. Before we look for a 'usable past' we ought to know *all* of the past." The responsibility to document and care for public memory often falls to BIPOC community arts sites through curation, production, and collection management. Doing so provides an alternative to the extractive archival practices of museum and library collections of empire (Azoulay 2020). Sometimes community archives are managed by the sites themselves, and other times in collaboration with external libraries. Diana Taylor (2007) writes that it is important to archive performance along with literary or visual culture. The act of participatory archiving itself can have positive educational outcomes through intergenerational exchange.

In addition to formal archival practices, such as evolving metadata and technological requirements, artistic practice can have memory devices woven into community participation. For example, Amiri Baraka riffed lists of names as a kind of spoken word bibliography of artists and activists that he wanted everyone to remember. Traditional capoeira ladainhas sing memories of people and places before each roda so practitioners remember their origins. Creative practices can counteract the invisibility and misrepresentation reinforced by what hooks (1984) terms "white supremacy capitalist patriarchy." Instead, feeling seen and heard can spark awareness of legacy, continuity, belonging, and even hope. Cahaus (2020) writes that Latine feminist geographies can create "spaces of mutual support, hope, healing, and love" (1). Adrienne Marie Brown's (2019) vision for leadership centers facilitation, and joy as a guiding force for social change.

The Covid-19 pandemic disrupted the ability for communities to gather in place, yet memory plays a role in sustaining social cohesion. Even with social distancing, memory of place fortifies connections between people across digital platforms. "Place has a particularly strong role in memory," neuroscientist Donna Addis explains. "The future and the past seem to be somehow linked in the mind." With the discovery of a place cell, natural scientists confirm the connections between place, story, and emotion in the brain (Knierim 2009). Addis's argument (as a natural scientist) harmonizes with Fuentes' perspective (as a novelist) linking the past, future, and present. She argues that connection to place "weaves together memories of the past and your dreams for the future to create your sense of self" (Vox 2019).

Expressions of participation and leadership in BIPOC cultural spaces are often inspired by community cherishing. Cherishing self and community is expressed in action through art making, mentorship, labor, and volunteerism. Over time, even as roles within art spaces shift and change, intergenerational relationships spawn bonds of kinship that can shift, endure, and inspire. Enduring intergenerational relationships of connection and mentorship were continuously mentioned as a key leadership style during the focus group. BIPOC community arts sites play important roles connecting generations across culture and place while cultivating creative courage and action.

GATHERING

The focus group allowed everyone to come together in the same space. As people arrived, Caldwell commented on the spatial similarities: a Gold Line rail stop directly across from Self Help Graphics, a Crenshaw line stop opening up facing Leimert Park Village, and another new stop under construction catty corner to Visual Communications. We shared a meal prepared by Moni Vegan, a Latina owned culinary business run by a local artist and entrepreneur committed to wellness. She served up a delicious vegetarian spin on enchiladas and ensalada with a refreshing fruit drink of agua de melón. When we arrived to help set up the space, Self Help Graphics's youth arts initiative, Soy Artista, was guiding an art making workshop in the central studio. Young artists were adorning calaveras for the upcoming Day of the Dead festivities. Ofelia Esparza, a master artist and National Endowment of the Arts National Heritage Fellow, was preparing an intricate, colorful altar with her daughter Rosanna Ahrens. The action research team joined in the fun by twirling and pinning orange paper marigolds — cempasúchitl in the Nahuatl language — that transformed pillars into a floral oasis, while Avila and Reva Santo set up the sound and video equipment for documentation.

This moment captures the unique qualities that make community arts spaces so vital to any arts and cultural ecosystem. They are intergenerational creative spaces that affirm, transmit, and renew local culture and creativity, permeable sites for gathering, mentorship, cultural preservation, wellness, education, and reinvention. They are spaces where people can connect, create, learn, and imagine.

Avila Santo set a microphone stand in the center of the gallery, and we curved folding chairs into a circle to face each other. The documentarians moved freely among the group as we spoke and listened. We began by introducing ourselves, our affiliations, and why we were present. I reshared the themes for discussion, and arts management students introduced each topic to kick off the conversations.

Intergenerational circle at Self Help Graphics. Photo: Reva Santo

WELCOME TO THE CIRCLE

The circle gathered intergenerational arts leaders of color from the east side to the south side. Ben Caldwell had been living in the Leimert Park neighborhood since 1984. "I run a place that's called Kaos Network," he said. "I'm loving to see what the changes are going to be. I run toward change as opposed to running away from it." Caldwell is an African American filmmaker who cut his teeth during the Black cinematic movement called the L.A. Rebellion. Betty Avila, born and raised in Northeast Los Angeles, is the Executive Director of Self Help Graphics. She was interested in "conversations about how we're building power, how we're building wealth and long-term sustainability for the organization, which then has ripple effects in the community around us and the community that we serve." She said that Boyle Heights had been the center of attention around gentrification and looked forward to connecting with colleagues finding themselves in similar situations across the city. "Many of our peers have dealt with this or are tackling similar issues," she said. Joel Garcia, from Lakeside, is an artist who was co-directing Self Help Graphics at the time of the gathering. He was interested in how to best steward space. "Whether it's land or a theoretical space that we put into practice," he said, "and how we exchange with one another — whether it's through commerce or ideas, through the internet or teaching." Alexa Kim, also of Self Help Graphics, served as the organization's program coordinator.

Kim Harris was a Leimert Park homeowner. "I moved back into my house in Leimert Park," she said, "and I am so glad I did. I have a great sense of community." Kimberly Osorio, of the action research team, said, "I was born and raised in South L.A. ... My part of the research project has to do with land and ownership of land for people of color... [and how this] affected arts organizations from staying in one place."

"I'm an East L.A. native," Miranda Ynez said, "born and raised in Boyle Heights." An Afro-Latinx arts manager on the action research team, Ynez said, "I am honored and inspired to be here with you all." To her right sat Lucy Lu, a purple-haired, arts manager from Beijing, China on the team. Next to her was Brittany Fields, an African American visual artist and arts manager who moved to Los Angeles from St. Louis. Alma Catalan grew up in Boyle Heights and returned to complete her degree in arts management the following year. "The "first opportunity I had to access the arts was through Self Help Graphics," she said. "Back when I was in high school…but it was at the old building. I'm feeling honored to be here at the new space and to be part of this conversation." Self Help Graphics already had to relocate once. The harsh reality of displacement sparked their desire not to be displaced again. Since that time, Self Help Graphics & Art purchased their building and became, according to Betty Avila, one of four Latine arts organizations in the country that own their space.

Francis Cullado, Director of Visual Communications, came to the meeting from Little Tokyo. "I was born in the Philippines," he said, "I came here, and grew up in Long Beach." He is an important arts and culture leader and advocate. "I always think about L.A. in terms of neighborhoods and places," he said. "If I wasn't doing this [directing Visual Communications], I wanted to get my Ph.D. in human geography. We always talk about diversity and inclusivity. Yes, L.A. is diverse, but still segregated, and sometimes we kind of do that to ourselves because we get stuck in our own silos too."

Jilly Canizares, immigrated to Los Angeles from the Philippines and went on to become a respected leader of FilAm Arts. "I am currently working with Policy Link on a community development initiative to combine community development with the arts," she said. Yolanda Hester, an African American oral historian, said that she has focused on "community development, and economic and enterprise activities within black communities."

I introduced myself last, explaining that we had visited everyone's spaces and wanted to convene everyone together with the student team and document the conversation. As a matter of process, I wanted everyone to be able to share out face-to-face, and for students to confirm the accuracy of their assumptions. "I'm here because I have a background in the arts and in community arts," I said. 'Right now, I am a professor in a university. So, this is a role that I would like our program to have — being connected, being supportive, and being a place for people to grow."

LAND

Osorio had combed through maps and archives to reveal social, cultural, and creative tensions related to the theme of land. During the focus group, she spoke to benchmarks in local history including the Tongva Nation's indigenous roots in the area, the Mexican period of Los Angeles prior to the Treaty of Guadalupe Hidalgo, the internment of Japanese Americans, and how anti-immigrant and redlining policies denied people of color the right to own homes and businesses. Osorio concluded that the legal system "prohibited people of color from even purchasing or owning land." She turned to the group. "What is your vision of ownership and stewardship of land?" she said. Was it important to own one's own space or were pop-up activities enough?

"Linda Mabalot [one of Visual Communications' former Executive Directors] fought hard for us to get this place," Cullado said. For 20 years, Visual Communications' office has been in the Union Center for the Arts in Little Tokyo. The space provides a home for Pan-Asian arts organizations including East West Players. The space is co-managed by the Little Tokyo Service Center and was formerly the old Union Church, a site where Japanese Americans were taken before and (after internment) when President Roosevelt issued Executive Order 9066 in February of 1942. The Union Center for the Arts is adjacent to the Japanese American National Museum that was founded much later, in 1992. Little Tokyo Service Center (LTSC) is a non-profit community development organization whose mission is to "provide a comprehensive array of social welfare and community development services to assist low-income individuals...contribute to community revitalization and cultural preservation in Little Tokyo."

"That is our home," Cullado said, "but I never want to equate home with ownership." In his situation, Visual Communications found stability with an affordable, long-term lease arrangement. "This is really complex," Cullado said, regarding local preservation efforts to "Keep Little Tokyo Little Tokyo." Heated negotiations were taking place over whether the Parker Center, a former police station, merited preservation. "The city demolished one-quarter of Little Tokyo to build Parker Center and then turned its back end to the community," said Yukio Kawaratani during comments in a public hearing. The Parker Center was eventually demolished. Historic preservation and neighborhood revitalization efforts must ask the question: whose history is being remembered, and whose history is being left out?

Caldwell had fond memories of collaborating with Linda Mabalot, Abe Ferrer, and Bob Nakamura who founded Visual Communications, and enjoyed reminiscing about them. He said,

> The 60's children were kind of forced to work together...It was a full right movement with everything that we did, so even Leimert Park — because Brockman Gallery was there...You know, we had [the band] Hiroshima in the house as a part of it, and we had Bobby Matos [a salsero] in the house as a part of all of what we did along with our African Film Festivals and things like that.

Caldwell's memories of intercultural collaboration in the arts were tied to social movements. "I think as an African American community," he said, "…We were always multicultural. We dealt with everybody as if they were our family…Even though we're a black community, we're only 9 percent of the population…Within that, we've worked with everybody in a real strong way."

"If we possess the land," Ben Caldwell said, "we can become erasure proof." He was pleased that art spaces in Leimert Park had prioritized ownership. There is a legacy of black home ownership in the neighborhood, however there is also a strong push to sell family homes given the financial returns. One way or another, staving off gentrification would require sustaining black space. "I think we've won the job of owning the property," Caldwell said. "Now it is on what do you do once that happens?" He spoke about the difficulty black families had purchasing View Park properties to begin with, but "the youth are selling their property because they want to go to other places…You know, you get offered a million dollars, and then you sell out, because it was only worth about $300,000 before." This dynamic in Leimert Park was distinct from what was happening in Boyle Heights on the east side where renting predominates, or Little Tokyo with little residential stock remaining of Asian Pacific Islander families. Caldwell spoke about blackness as deeply rooted in Los Angeles. "The thing that we forget," he said, "is that black has been indigenous." The first city census reveals that black people of Mexico were among the first pobladores of the City of Los Angeles.

Caldwell described the wave of gentrification as something that was rising for decades. "A lot of us have been working for the last 20 years on the idea that gentrification was happening," he said. "We had these early morning meetings … because the real community goes there every Monday." Caldwell equated black cultural resiliency with community organizing among residents, small minority owned businesses (MOBs), and arts and cultural organizations who met, built trust, and strategized together for local sustainability. He referred to the incoming Metro rail line and station as an undeniable disruptor. "Before the crisis happened," Caldwell said, "even before the vision of the Metro coming in, we were dealing with the issues of how to deal with our neighborhood." Transportation studies have found that the Metro rail line expansion exacerbated gentrification and displacement in Los Angeles (Zuk, et al., 2015). The University of California study blamed this negative impact on a lack of adequate ordinances to protect affordable housing and small business. Rail expansion was a common concern in each of the three neighborhoods represented in the room: the Gold Line coming through Little Tokyo and Boyle Heights, and the new Crenshaw green line that will connect the Expo line to the Los Angeles Airport running through South L.A. along Crenshaw Boulevard.

When the Crenshaw Line build began, it triggered a series of environmental and social concerns among residents. "It was tearing down trees," Caldwell said. "The community had to figure out deals and what we wanted." Community members banded together to help resolve problems. "The first thing we figured out was how to deal with the trees," he said. Neighbors asked to repurpose the felled trees to make useful things like drums or art. They also negotiated "a five to one replacement for them." For every tree that was cut down, they would plant more. In addition to the aesthetic benefits, trees "play an important role in the global carbon cycle by absorbing carbon dioxide during photosynthesis, storing carbon above and below ground, and producing oxygen as a by-product of photosynthesis." (U.S. Department of Agriculture).

Community organizing is necessary for local residents to engage with power structures during redevelopment. Some people might call this a struggle or a fight. "I'm not trying to use war words." As a filmmaker and former veteran, Caldwell said,

> We should figure out how to make things happen artistically, because we're not warriors in the sense of using guns. We're

artists that have a lot more power than guns. I think we should utilize that as opposed to always talking war syndromes.

Similarly, to Caldwell having positive memories of Visual Communications, Joel Garcia wanted everyone to know that Kaos Network had welcomed Latinx musicians from the east side into Project Blowed. "A very interesting connection that folks might not know about," Garcia said, "is Kaos Network and Boyle Heights." Access to space is a major issue for young artists who need places to create and find refuge. "For a lot of young musicians in Boyle Heights [Kaos Network] was that place through Project Blowed." He remembered Project Blowed as "a gathering of brilliant minds." Garcia affirmed Caldwell's interpretation of black space as inclusive. Kaos Network also made him think about how one might go about owning or curating an art space in the future.

Garcia described Self Help Graphics as a site for creation of visual art, intellectual thought, music, poetry, and theater. These positive outcomes were possible due to having "a space to congregate and come together." How can one even imagine having or curating a space when "there's no money, there's just nothing," Garcia said, "Nothing to grasp." He spoke about the loss of Self Help Graphics' first building — a spacious, mosaic-lined building off of Cesar Chavez Avenue. The original site boasted office space, exhibition space, classrooms, a welding studio, and an enormous parking lot that was regularly transformed into an art marketplace. Neighbors enjoyed the annual Day of the Dead parade that kicked off at a local taco shop and filled the streets with larger-than-life *titere* puppets, costumed *calacas*, and exciting festivities.

While the original space felt like home, they never owned the deed to the property. When SHG lost authority over the space "it was really the community that took agency around taking ownership of the organization," said Garcia. The community inspired the organization to "talk about land ownership…to talk about buying property, to talk about justice."

Community attention went beyond one site to include social and environmental issues impacting the community at large. The loss of trees and location of public spaces became sources of contention and community organizing. Garcia alluded to the redevelopment of Tongva Park, and disputes over the L.A. River that runs between the Arts District and Boyle Heights. Today, the L.A. River runs between two different communities. He said,

> We rebuilt the new park along the river…The whole contention there was like, well if it becomes too much Boyle Heights, the folks on the West side of the river are going to have an issue about it. If it becomes too much of the Arts District, then we're forgetting about the folks in Boyle Heights.

Inspired by the Zapatista movement, Garcia recited, "the land belongs to those who work it." Self Help Graphics recommitted to the stewardship of land and culture and successfully went about purchasing their building to help anchor the community and not be displaced again. "In many ways," Garcia said, "we're doing the work that a farmer does to keep this land fertile, to keep this space fertile."

Ben Caldwell speaks with students about his legacy and projects. Photo: Author.

*Chanel Kong and Abe Ferrer speak with students about
the legacy of Visual Communications. Photo: Author.*

STORY

June Jordan's notion of "space cherishing" came through the stories told about neighborhood and cultural space in the circle. "I grew up in East L.A.," said Miranda Ynez. "The arts and culture here have helped shape who I am and what I believe in. It really is a painting of my existence." Disturbed by the forces of gentrification that stalked her neighborhood, she asked the group: "What are your own personal stories of sustainability in the face of displacement?"

Cullado explained that Visual Communications' work emphasizes storytelling. "Our [art] form is storytelling through film, whether it is place-based, or characters based on that place…We want to build an army of media makers to tell our place-based stories." While Caldwell rejects "war words," no feathers were ruffled by Cullado's reference to an army of visual storytellers. It was clear that he meant preparing a multitude. Cullado expressed concern about changes to the built environment in Little Tokyo, including the new Metro rail stop, the safety of elderly Japanese Americans living in Keiro housing, and artists who had been evicted from the Arts District and 800 Traction. "People," he said, "no longer feel like they're safe."

He was also proud of Visual Communications's efforts to tell intercultural, historically rich stories representing place. They completed a project on Bronzeville, Little Tokyo — a time during internment when the neighborhood was populated by black and brown families, including the notorious jazz artist Charlie Parker. The film project required extensive historical research. "We still don't have the full stories that were really happening after internment, when people came back into the neighborhood," he noted. What happens when people are forced to leave but want to come back?

Cullado commented on his experiences working in Little Tokyo and Historic Filipinotown. "Little Tokyo is more organized," he said. People care deeply about the sustainability of the community. As an observer, I was impressed by the collaborative approach used in Little Tokyo and the role that the Little Tokyo Service Center plays as a backbone organization in a neighborhood with numerous cultural anchors.

Canizares has been a catalytic arts leader in Los Angeles. Many Filipino and Filipino American arts leaders cut their teeth working on the annual Festival of Philippine Arts and Culture (FPAC) and have gone on to hold leadership positions in numerous cultural organizations throughout the region. "The movement to name Historic Filipinotown," she said, "started about 50 years ago or more." The effort was complicated by the fact they had to "gain common ground among a multilingual diasporic community…The only way we got the designation Filipino Town, was when we named it historic."

Shaping the narrative about one's culture and community is a powerful act. One narrative shift mentioned was related to the stewardship of land. The narrative shifts to stewardship brought a positive energy to the debate about renting or owning space. This notion came from the Zapatista movement ideal in Chiapas, Mexico (Chiapas Media Project 2005). Changes in nomenclature were also voiced by Caldwell. As a veteran, he rejected "war words" such as fight and struggle. Instead he preferred using artistic words that emphasized social action as a creative process.

Cullado explained "disjointedness" as an obstacle to "actually move forward together." Sensitivity to intersectionality was expressed in an inclusive approach to leadership development, curation and programming. Consider Visual Communications' annual Pan-Asian Film Festival, or Self Help Graphic's highlighting non-binary artists in their exhibitions and events such as Paper Fashion Gala and Runway Show.

"Francis," Betty Avila said to Cullado. "You said something earlier about how you don't want to equate home with property ownership."

That resonated. She grew up in Cypress Park, in Northeast L.A., and had a powerful sense of belonging even though she hadn't been a homeowner. Renters also feel a keen sense of belonging and commitment to place. "I think about a lot of the spaces or places that we grew up around that make up a part of our story, but are not necessarily positive," Betty Avila said. She questioned why one might feel nostalgic about preserving places like liquor stores, gas stations, or places where illicit things happen. Certainly, not all history merits preservation. "I recently ... went to a photography exhibition," she said. "One of the photographs blown up really beautifully was the façade of the sweat shop where my mother used to work." She had a visceral reaction to the photos in the exhibition. I walked in... 'Oh my god!' It literally felt like a punch in the stomach. On one hand... this is a place where my mom sustained us and basically supported her family, but, at the same time, it's also not necessarily the most positive memory...This place is across the street from lofts, artists' lofts, and I think it still serves the purpose of a garment factory. I feel really conflicted about it. Do I want this place to stay?"

She spoke powerfully about the extractive economies that make up a part of local histories and asked us to consider what deserves preservation, and how the arts might better address the complex human stories of our families and neighborhoods. After 45 years of creative programming, Betty Avila believed that preserving Self Help Graphics was of paramount importance. Purchasing a building is "a very big step," she said. "To purchase this building and to give it a permanent home, that's a huge value statement." She connected the organization's stability with the longevity and resiliency of Latinx communities in the neighborhood and region.

Librarian Sal Güëreña archives "Noche de Poesía"
by Christopher Ramirez in the CEMA archives. Photo: Author.

Box set of <u>Asian American People and Places: Ethnic Understanding Series</u>, Visual Communications.

MEMORY

Each organization in the circle had an open-source strategy for hosting archival materials online to make them easily accessible to the public. They also, however, negotiated arrangements with well-resourced institutions, including university and public archives, sometimes far away from their locales. The benefit to inclusion in educational archives included positioning artists and communities of color in archival metadata. Art based archives include multimedia knowledge objects and require different kinds of care and technology to maintain. The variety of formats pose technological challenges for preservation. "Imagine," said Cullado, "old tapes, old film, and it just takes so much time and energy just to digitize things."

Proximity, quality, and accessibility were key values identified for archival work. Brittany Fields was interested in archives as a powerful way to bring attention to communities of color, and for informing contemporary marketing campaigns. With a background in printmaking and photography, Fields became fascinated with preserving memory through accessible art archives. "I'm a non-native of L.A., Fields said, "so I've been introduced to a lot of organizations through social media and internet research — your digital footprint." She saw how archives "collect the stories of the community." Fields asked the group, "How are you documenting and archiving these stories, and what are you doing once you actually have them in your possession?

Cullado said that Visual Communication's founders valued building an institutional archive that was locally accessible and community oriented. They use their archive for both preservation and exhibition. Recently, highlights from their archive were shown at the Japanese American National Museum in an exhibition called *At First Light: The Dawning of Pacific Asian America*. "There's a lot of looking back," Cullado said. Visual Communications consults their historical archive to analyze high stakes struggles for the future. He mentioned that universities, such as UCLA and Duke, had approached Visual Communications about digitization. He wanted to amplify Asian Pacific Islander artists, honor the intellectual property rights of artists, and make sure the materials are cared for properly. "My warm moments are somebody that's walking down First Street, and then they see a mural or a photo, and someone goes, "Oh. That's my Grandpa!"

Fields had noticed a shift in Self Help Graphics' social media efforts. "Where it was mostly just photos, and then you [added] interviews of current, younger people, and then the older patrons of your organization," she said. Their website featured displays of artworks, interviews, histories, and events. Alexa Kim confirmed. "What Brittany is referring to was kind of to ramp up for our Pacific Standard Time exhibition, but, also, our 45th anniversary… followed shortly by a 50th anniversary." Alexa Kim said,

> We are a print archive. We have many, many prints that have been created through Self Help Graphics studios over many years. Our formal archive does live up at U.C. Santa Barbara, which some of you have visited. The UCSB archive is far away from here…It was the third collection to be acquired by [Center for Ethnic and Multicultural Art] CEMA back in the early 90s.

"For us, each one of these prints is a story," Garcia chimed in. "It's a reflection of what was happening in the community at the time through the interpretation of an artist."

Self Help Graphics makes annual pilgrimages with staff, and youth interns, to CEMA during the summers. They invited me and Brittany Fields to join them in the van. The benefit of inclusion in CEMA is that pieces are housed in state-of-the-art archival facilities, and that the works can be used by students, faculty, and alumni at

UCSB for exhibitions, teaching, and research. While CEMA is miles away from Boyle Heights, they expand the ring of community geographically. "From what we know," Alexa Kim said, "that archive is visited on a weekly basis by other artists, academics, so it's good to know that the work that went into the preservation of those prints - even as far away as they are — there's access to it."

Self Help Graphics has also digitized works in open-source format for the broader public. "We've been spending the last five years digitizing the work, so now it's accessible to everybody," said Garcia. He said,

> With these prints, with this database, with this collection, the open source-ism of information is something that...allow(s) more conversations and world dialogues to happen through every print. We have close to 1,000 of these, so you can imagine the amount of information that can be attached to each single one.

The hope was that the combination of using CEMA (a university archive), and their own open-source digital archive, would increase recognition of Chicanx / Latinx artists worldwide.

Betty Avila said that the CEMA archives were founded due to the activism of a Latinx librarian Sal Guereña. "What if Sal [Güereña] hadn't been at U.C. Santa Barbara, and you didn't have this woke Chicano librarian coming to meet with Sister Karen [Boccalero, Founder of Self Help Graphics and Art]? Güereña used his position as a University of California librarian to highlight artists of color in the UC system. She saw the value of having different kinds of archival spaces. Using a university run archive can be "a double-edged sword." On one hand, "I love the fact that all of Self Help's stuff lives in this very climate-controlled, beautiful drawer situation, but it also feels a little bit like it's in prison..." Participating in the impressive CEMA archive, while also managing their own local archive for residents, allowed them to best serve their different communities.

Betty Avila was enthusiastic about the video oral history project. She said,

> What I loved is that they were done by our college interns. They are done by young people, who are interpreting these histories. They did an amazing job...We have also a cohort of high school and college students who we train to give tours of this exhibition, so that when we have high school students and elementary school students coming in, they're hearing about this story and this history from someone not that far from who they are.

This approach generated positive learning outcomes for youth, sparked intergenerational exchange, and expanded their online archive. "I think that it's really important," she said, "that we think about who's being empowered to share the stories, and then how we're documenting it, right? How accessible is that to our communities?"

Yolanda Hester explained that the oral histories she collects are often archived "far away from the people who are actually telling the story." The oral histories she collects highlight the ingenuity of black businesses. "Some of these businesses are 70 years old, 50 years old, and so anyone who listens would really learn a lot about how they've dealt with changes; demographic changes, policy changes, all sorts of changes that affect communities." She wanted to find ways to archive the oral histories closer to the places they came from.

Caldwell maintains a media archive at Kaos Network and archives his own artwork. For him, archiving work was a way to capture memories of a movement. The L.A. Rebellion's work is now archived at UCLA. He advocated for separating personal and institutional works to 1) preserve family ownership, autonomy, future rights and their related income, and 2) use institutional archives for pieces that merited a larger reach. "The major thing that I would suggest about archiving," Caldwell said, "is to get it outside of an institution, make it a private, controlled space…" He continued,

> To me, it's really good to be owned by yourself as much as possible." I'm keeping a lot of it open sourced, so the community can use it, but the stuff that's diamonds.
>
> I collect it myself, and my family, my daughters can make money from it, and my grandchildren can…

While he welcomed collaboration, Caldwell wanted to also make sure that people unaffiliated with a university could access the archive. Caldwell was enthusiastic about "things we can do" — action that is within one's reach. He developed a redesigned, rolling public telephone booth with the ability to receive and deposit stories. When you lift the receiver, the contraption projects Caldwell's voice over a speaker system and welcomes you to play along. It guides you into history in an immersive space. It's a lot of fun. He has repurposed and reinvented old technologies in new ways and makes archives into interactive works of art. The stories are archived in the artwork and on the internet. The memories "will be left there, but it will also be left in the overall internet world," he said.

An archive can reach beyond the local physical environment, or educational and arts institutions, to inform diasporic connections. McKittrick and Woods (2007) imagined black geographies that move "within and against the grain of dominant modes of power, knowledge, and space…" (2007, 5). One way that community art spaces reimagine, and challenge power is through diasporic connectivity. Woods wrote that "overlapping diasporic spaces are inflected with local matters and cultural expressions." (2007, 8). Community art spaces disrupt simplistic notions of belonging by uniting local and diasporic spaces through art. Caldwell was fascinated by modern technologies and experimenting with augmented (AR) and virtual reality (VR). "That's our way of going at the history…A little bit in the future, and then the present, and then really not forgetting the past."

Linda Vallejo, Calaca, and Betty Avila prep for Dia de Los Muertos at SHG.

Student site visit to Union Arts in Little Tokyo. Photos: Author.

LEADERSHIP

"When I hear the word Leadership," said Alma Catalan, "I think of mentorship...I was introduced to the arts through mentorship and was able to build my craft and be in an arts community." The community spaces that welcomed her into the arts were Self Help Graphics and Casa 0101 (founded by screenwriter and director Josefina Lopez). Over time, Catalan became an arts advocate and mentor. "I'm trying to build that agency among youth, so that they know that 'You know what? You can own your own story, right?" She looked around the circle and said, "You guys are leading the way."

Cullado said he gained his leadership education from the community itself. Cullado continued:

> I watch other people. How they do it. My professors, my parents, Jilly [Canizares] when she was running the Festival of Philippine Arts & Culture (FPAC), and how she's dealing with her people, and dealing with issues...I'm just really blessed to have a lot of good people around me.

His leadership vision prioritized team building, finding "other people to trust," and the financial resources to pay your team. "It's just really good to be in spaces where you understand you're just not alone." Canizares led FPAC for 15 years. Her approach emphasized leadership development and team building. "What I did, in order to produce something that kept growing, is to create a leadership team." Group facilitation was paramount. "Sometimes the most powerful person in the room," she said, "is the neutral one in allowing everybody to speak. The neutral one holds the space, so that all these voices can come out." Her approach was an alternative to hierarchical, top-down leadership structures. Canizares said,

I think we've been schooled by our colonizers that in the pyramid we're in, only one speaks, but I think by the nature of our multicultural environment in Los Angeles, it's necessary to have all those voices speak. That's where I met Amy, because we've been dealing with a lot of multicultural dynamics and leadership, not only here, but also in the state.

Canizares' vision for a "modern leader" in a "multicultural space" is "somebody who can negotiate that code switch…between generations and between cultures."

My relationship to Jilly Canizares grew from community organizing for multicultural arts at the state level, and had evolved into a lifetime of collaboration and friendship. As the focus group facilitator, I mostly listened and kept time. During the discussion on leadership, I chimed in. "What's on my mind a lot is self-leadership," I said. "I try to be authentic in the spaces that I have access to." As a head of household, leadership meant raising a family. Now, as a professor, leadership means making choices about knowledge, curriculum, people, and partnerships.

Caldwell developed his leadership style from his craft. He runs teams following the structure used by filmmakers. Each one of them has a director, producer, and all the line elements that are needed to complete their jobs, and they're completed at various times. That's how I ran Project Blowed, because I wasn't a hip-hopper, but I respected where they were coming from. He observed that each project pod would "have their own power system." He would serve as a "conduit between them. "My basis is the L.A. Rebellion," Caldwell said. Making art in a collective fashion influenced his view of arts management and ethical leadership. The process developed during the L.A. Rebellion worked for him, and he has refined it during the past thirty years. He said,

That template is by any means necessary, but not killing people, or hurting people, or disrespecting people, but every other way. That process is really a proper utilization of resources, and not to dream beyond what we had the capacity to do, but have it operate within the context of what you have.

Betty Avila said that mentorship is core to her leadership vision. "One of the very important things for me is mentorship, and being mindful and cognizant that mentorship goes in different directions, up and down. I learn a lot from the young people in this space, and I try to incorporate mentorship as a practice." She had been in formal mentor programs, but felt that mentorship was best "when it's really just part of the way that you work." She recalled having to demonstrate her capacities in each post that she has held, and hoped that organizations would give young leaders the opportunity to hold responsibility. She felt "hopeful that this is just the beginning of a trend."

"I've been told by multiple people you have to be an arts leader," said Miranda Ynez. "You have to be an arts leader; you have to be an arts leader. During my undergrad at UCLA, I was like, 'but there's no arts leader of color.' It wasn't until I got the Getty internship where I started connecting with people and other organizations" and was introduced to a small community of art leaders of color. "I want to give back to that," she said. "...I want to uplift other black and brown folks in our communities. So thank you for being here. I really appreciate it." Brittany Fields spoke next. "It is actually super great to see how all the organizations are interconnected in ways that I think people —you probably do know— but I was not privy to that."

Kim Harris said, "it's been nice to be here...You guys are some very interesting young people. Lead well and do what you can to end racism." The room became quiet. We heard her, and let the words sink in. Her sentence rattled inside us: "Lead well and do what you can to end racism."

It took more than one lifetime to invent racism, and it will take more than one lifetime to eradicate it. The two Kim's were sitting next to each other in the circle. Harris, an older African American community leader, and Osorio, a younger Latinx arts activist were both born and raised in South L.A. I looked at the younger Kim and nodded. *Anything to add?* She raised her arms in a question mark and laughed. *How do you follow that? What more could be said?* The task at hand was ending racism and xenophobia.

"Sure," Osorio grinned sarcastically: "We'll do it!"

Laughter was our shared punctuation mark. The conversation concluded pinned to Harris' aspirational wish. We folded and stacked chairs, circled the audio cable, and poured from the gallery back into the central space. Ofelia Esparza's altar stretched out along the northern wall, cloaked with marigolds and photographs, bread for the dead, and handmade mementos to inspire the living. We spread out around the altar to admire its richness.

Alexa Kim prepares artworks for inclusion in the CEMA Archive.

Musicians gather at the World Stage in Leimert Park. Photos: Author.

FINAL REFLECTIONS

Erasure Proof found that BIPOC community arts sites generate important ecologies of culture and place. These ecologies contribute to the quality of life —what Escobar (2018) calls el Buen Vivir)— and the understanding of who and where we are. The stories conveyed in this essay exemplify cherishing community through creative social endurance: resilience that is grounded in adaptation, connection, and care. The ability for communities to adapt to crises requires unfathomable endurance (Ruiz 2019). "Humans, especially humans who persist in trying to transform the conditions of life, are remarkably resilient" writes Brown (2017). In addition to generating arts and culture with a local and diaspora reach, the sites position BIPOC arts and culture in broader efforts for community self-determination, dignity in housing, equitable development, restorative justice, mobility and transportation alternatives, and access to greenspace.

Since the time we spent together, Cullado and Visual Communications shared their social movement origin story through an exhibition *At First Light: The Dawning of Asian Pacific America* at the Japanese American Museum. SHG decided to purchase their building as an expression of public commitment to Latinx arts and cultural programming in the area. Caldwell and Kaos Network remain leading voices fostering black creative space in South Los Angeles and have led efforts to bring bike and electric public mobility options to the neighborhood. Campbell went on to work in college admissions increasing access to higher education in the arts. Ynez went on to help SHG envision and launch a new Youth Leadership Committee and served as a community arts organizer with the LA Commons in South Los Angeles. Catalan returned to complete her degree and now manages a community arts education program at a local university. Even the focus group documentarians have grown their creative work (A. Santo 2019; R. Santo 2021). This essay is an expression of my ongoing commitment to writing, teaching, and honoring people and place.

Shortly after the project concluded, I attended an art feria that SHG hosts each winter. A DJ throttled music, and poets read aloud while artisanal vendors sold colorful prints, homemade t-shirts, jewelry, and ceramics. The husk of a sweet tamale warmed my hands as I walked through the upbeat space. I huddled by the atolito vendor with SHG staff to chat about their successful acquisition of the building and asked if our time together had made any difference. They nodded in agreement, "It helped us think." I blew into my cup of hot champurrado, grateful.

MIGRATIONS

Reva Mucha, seagulls, and interrogation testimony. Collage: Author.

My Grandma Was a Radical

Everything comes from somewhere, even me. As a child of immigrants, I've always been curious about where we came from, how we got here, and if we fit in. The struggle to read, write, and belong has been mixed up inside my head for as long as I can remember. Before I could write, I'd scribble lines on paper, push the scrawl up towards my father's face, and ask, "What does this say?" When I started learning to read in school at five years old, I knew from the pictures in our first-grade books that my family wasn't like the family in *Fun with Dick and Jane*. The book mom had tamed blonde hair, and her body was disciplined inside a lean pencil skirt. Was there something wrong with us if we were different? I assumed so.

I've always wondered whether or not I belonged here. Could I call myself an American? What does being American mean? Learning about my grandma Reva Mucha helped me answer questions like: where do I come from? How does my family fit in? What are we? Who am I? The easy stuff. Even if you believe in the idea of participatory democracy, history teaches us that it's not always easy to feel like you belong to America.

Grandma Reva was a Jew in a Christian world. She was a woman in a man's world. She was a Communist in a capitalist world. She was an immigrant in a xenophobic world. She was a pianist in a world of attorneys. She was a librarian in an anti-intellectual world. She was a multi-lingual in an English-only world. She was a peace activist in a warring world. She lived through pogroms, the Great Depression, the Holocaust, the Cold War, and (more happily) the ascension of organized labor and the Civil Rights Movement. She also lived through interrogation by the House Un-American Activities Committee (HUAC) and was followed for over a decade by FBI secret agents. She lost two homes — one during the Great Depression, and another from being blacklisted — and the stress of being under surveillance aggravated her health. She birthed and raised two sons, and experienced two marriages — the first to an immigrant Jew from a shtetl in the Austro-Hungarian Empire, and the second to an immigrant gentile from Poland, a chemist who invented lemon pepper. She moved west, collected driftwood, and became a community organizer. She began her life falling into the Black Sea and ended it with her ashes sprinkled over the Pacific Ocean.[1]

Young Reva Mucha in New Jersey.

My dad planted the seed of curiosity about his mother in me when he put me to bed at night. Instead of reading me books, he would tell me about his mom. Listening to him made me feel connected. I came from him, and he came from her. Even as a little bean pod of a girl, I was a part of that continuity. I hope that some of her chutzpah is circulating through me at the microscopic level.

Baby Reva with her sisters Sonya and Lisa in Kherson.

Reva was born on November 10, 1905, to Bessie Striker and Piotr Mucha in a shtetl called Kherson, in present day Ukraine. History and nationality are complicated subjects for Jewish people since we've been nomads, political borders have often shifted, and we spent periods of time stateless. I'll be simple. Reva was born on planet Earth at the following coordinates: 46°35'N, 32°35'E. When she was about eight, she crossed the Atlantic Ocean on a ship with her parents and two sisters, Sonya and Lisa. They landed at Ellis Island and forged a fresh life in New Jersey. They joined a progressive temple led by Rabbi Joachim Prinz, who spoke at the March on Washington for civil rights in 1963.[2] Facing history is a constant, creative act. I just marched with my children at the Women's March on Washington and demonstrated at the Los Angeles Airport against the Muslim ban last night.) After witnessing suffering during the pogroms, the Great Depression and the rise of fascism, she became radicalized to end poverty and fight for peace and justice. [3]

Reva died of Leukemia six months after I was born. She was busy dying while I was busy being born. Jews name newcomers after our ancestors. Reva inspired an ocean of R's in our family that followed in her wake. My middle initial. My brother's middle initial. The name of my brother's carpentry business. My daughter's first name, Reva. My brother's son's name, Reave. My family wanted Grandma Reva to be remembered, even though the details of her life were often hushed.

Some of Reva's stuff is still around me, too. Her second husband used to slip me little things she liked when I was a kid: a wooden nutcracker, a Mexican silver belt, pencils designed to wear like necklaces, a chorus of red birds painted on a brown silk wooden fan.

Over the years, I've collected random artifacts about her. I possess her driver's license, seven parched obituaries, a box of old photos, FBI documents, newspaper articles, photographs from the Los Angeles Herald Examiner, a personal letter addressed to her from the office of W.E.B. Dubois, and a transcript of her testimony before HUAC.

My dad layered her obituaries into squares the size of dumpling wrappers, like square wontons waiting to be filled. He stapled them together in the upper left corner, and paper- clipped them to her Kaiser Permanente card, driver's license, and my birth announcement. My daughter Reva found the envelope in a file cabinet one day when we were preparing for my dad's funeral. He died in Los Angeles on Independence Day in 2015 with his mouth open and fireworks exploding all around his quiet body. I opened the envelope, folded back the leaves of Reva's obituaries, and read. They all began the same way: Beloved Comrade. They're cropped too close to read the names of the newspaper outlets. One obituary describes her as "a partisan of peace and champion of improved relations between the United States and the Soviet Union." Another says that her life was "simple, but full of meaning." Another wrote that her death was "a heavy blow...May her death serve to bring us all to think of this troubled world in a more understanding way... and [achieve] peace among all nations." Each obituary is marked with a hand-drawn square in thick red pencil, like butchers used to mark the price of a piece of meat after it had been cut, weighed, and wrapped in white paper. The red lines must be my dad's markings. Having her artifacts pinned to my birth announcement for decades stapled me to her story. Grandma Reva is my ancestral root to American radicalism, and Jewish womanhood. She was pro-peace, pro-international friendship, anti-poverty, anti-racism, and anti-war. These values flow through my family and I hold them at my core.[4]

I have visual proof that we once were together in the same place at the same time, a black and white photo from 1965. In the shot, I'm a three-month old sitting on her lap. I was at a small square table with both of my grandmothers, Frida Rascha (who raised her family in Jerusalem), and Reva Mucha (who settled in Los Angeles, California). The table is bare except for two empty, family-sized bottles of generic cola. Reva is looking into my eyes and coaxing me to chat, but she died before I learned how to talk. All of our communication has been, well, posthumous.

History is mostly empty spaces. My ancestors are a part of the emptiness in vast outer space. We're a part of that thick dark matter that doesn't get written about and is easily forgotten. I wish I could read writing from women in my family tree. We weren't writers. Neither tradition, nor society, believed it was a good idea for us to write. They distinguished themselves in their own ways. My maternal Grandma was known for her kneidlach. She may have had a third-grade education. My mom attended agriculture school where she majored in bee keeping and animal husbandry. "If I get one more bee sting, I will die!" she used to say. Mom chose to express herself in imagery and became a visual artist. There are few traces of our existence on paper. "Jews weren't allowed to attend school," Reva's first husband told me. He was raised in a Jewish shtetl called Pitkamien in the Astro-Hungarian Empire. Boys went to the rabbi's house to study Torah, and girls were kept at home to do the chores. "Lunch was a crust of bread," he said. "You rubbed a clove of garlic on it for flavor."[5]

Reva was an anomaly among the women in my family, not because of her values or zeal for life, but because of the opportunities she fought for and took into her own hands. She went to school. She even attended her local university, Rutgers, where she earned a juris doctorate. This woman never practiced law. She was a pianist. But she wanted to learn, and she had to live at home while she was in school. Law was the only local program available.

One day, it occurred to me that I might have some homemade, written-down sentences in my family tree. I remembered Reva's testimony before HUAC. If I could find her testimony before the committee, I could read words and phrases in her own voice. Thank you, World Wide Web. Thank you, Google. Thank you, Freedom of Information Act (FOIA). Sure enough, I found the transcript from Reva's senate court hearing online. The proceedings are a real life play about power. I sat down on the couch with my son, and we read the cross-examination aloud. He read the part of his great grandmother. I played the interrogators. Digitized from a thick, red, hardcover book generated by the Government of the United States, the story begins:

Mr. Tavenner: "What is your name please?"

Grandma: "Reva Mucha Zwolinski."

The next day, I retyped Reva's interrogation into Word, preserving the original formatting: the capitals, the indentations, and the margins. This unleashed something in my imagination, and I set out hunting for more. I found photos of her from the hearing, and the 1952 World Trade Week in Los Angeles. I was thrilled to find these artifacts that brought her closer to me in a brand-new way. The research made me feel electric. I was lit up, ecstatic, a time traveler, proud, scared, disheartened, and sometimes angry. Grandma had been through so much. I looked up the names, photos and biographies of the HUAC Committee interrogators. I wanted to know their names and backgrounds. I tried to imagine what it was like to be Reva for a moment, but the whole thing seemed surreal. Could I piece together the parts I was finding to write something coherent, something true?

It is 1958. Los Angeles, California. A row of white men sit behind a long heavy table. Their suits are winter black. Everything else is gray — the towering ceilings, the swarm of journalists, tripods, and cameras. The space is packed with men dressed in wool wearing spectacles and Fedora hats. Their thin ties are knotted with confidence around their necks and adorned with metal clips inscribed with their initials, ebony stones, or fish bone diamonds. The room reverberates with garbled conversation. The courtroom is a container for rumbling. Voices float up to the ceiling and bang against the crown moldings that form a barrier to the sky.

Reva walks into the dense, hair-slicked, crowd of white men wearing a purple and gold paisley blouse with a thin bow looped at the neckline. She sits in a wooden chair beside her counsel, John T. McTernan.

A gavel smacks against hard wood. Conversations cease. Reva faces the table of suits constituting the committee: Francis E. Walter of Pennsylvania, Morgan M. Moulder of Missouri, Clyde Boyle and Donald L. Jackson of California, Edwin Willison of Louisiana, William M. Tuck of Virginia, Bernard W. Kearney of New York, Gordon H. Sherer of Ohio, Robert J. McIntosh of Michigan, and Mr. Frank S. Tavenner Jr., of Virginia. Tavenner, the U.S. Attorney for the District of Virginia, is Chief Counsel. He hails from the home of the World-Famous Skeeter Dog, and is the same guy who interrogated Pete Seeger, the folk singer.

Tavenner holds his sharpened pencil between his index and middle fingers and points the tip to the sky. The pocket on the blazer that cloaks his stocky build is jammed with ballpoint pens. His nose exists primarily to suspend his black-framed glasses because he has no sense of smell. He breathes, instead, through his mouth. His lips are a thin flat line. The chalky, church-abiding Southern man writes his name in solid block letters and lives each day with the utmost certainty that he, in fact, knows best. The daily experience of privilege has gotten to his head. His neck has grown as wide as his jaw.

Tavenner prefers his breakfast fried and takes his coffee light with lots of cream, but no damn sugar. He lives his professional life in a permanent state of disapproval, accumulating girth with each HUAC interrogation that he administers. Xenophobia has been his windfall. McCarthyism fills his belly by providing him with a steady stream of generous federal checks — good paper money — that he stashes away in a private account he believes (with every inch of his Anglo-Saxon heart) makes Jesus love him even more than he already did for being born white with an XY chromosome.

Tavenner's voice reverberates into a stainless-steel microphone the size of an eggplant. The sound system fills the corridors with the wailing echo of his drawl. Each of his questions is a setup, a door handle designed to lead the witness down a corridor to make the tables and chairs shrink to the size of a mushroom or grow as big as a house. An Un-American house. An American house. Same difference. The courtroom performance is real and surreal. The table could just as well have been cluttered with teapots and plates of cookies from Lewis Carroll's rabbit hole. A dormouse. A deck of cards. A mad hatter.

"Whooooo are you?" Tavenner says in the languid bellow of a hookah smoking larvae.

"I — I hardly know, sir, just at present," Reva says. "At least I know who I WAS when I got up this morning…" [6]

"Youuuuuu are a commie, pinko, Jew girl heretic."

"No, your honor," she says. "I'm a mother and grandmother. I completed my legal studies at Rutgers University. I was one of the few women in my class."

Tavenner scowls. "A woman's place is in the home."

"Sir, I lived at home with my parents during my university studies."

Tavenner raises his right arm. "Off with her head!"

"But Sir. I'm non-violent. I'm an advocate for peace and global exchange."

Tavenner ruffles through stacks of documents that resemble a small paper city before him. He manipulates the piles with his hands. He is building something.

How can I write accurately about history during such strange times? The committee believed it was their duty to demonize immigrants and Communism to defend their white supremacist vision of America. Jim Crow applauded the America they defended and believed in. Everything outside their vision of America was Un-American. They were defending the same America I learned to sound out in *Fun with Dick and Jane.* Should I candy coat it? Serve it up in a porcelain teacup and saucer with a silver spoon? Better to be honest. Jim Crow is Jim Crow.

Reva's testimony begins with Tavenner asking her name and origin. This was important to him because of the Smith Act. It had not yet been found unconstitutional. Congress passed the Smith Act in 1940 as the Alien Registration Act. This allowed the Congress to interrogate, harass, and even banish people they accused of being Communist sympathizers. Reva's interrogation was led by Tavenner and included questioning by Moulder and a man they called "The CHAIRMAN." Tavenner begins by asking Grandma to confirm her name and origin. She states her name but objects to talking about her birthplace.

"I don't believe that that question is actually pertinent to the questioning this afternoon, sir," Reva says.

The committee's intention was to shame her as a foreign born Communist. If they did so, the Alien Act of 1940, also called the Smith Act, gave them permission to extradite her even though she'd lived in the United States since she was a small girl.

Mr. TAVENNER: "May I have a direction that the witness answer the question as to where she was born?"

The CHAIRMAN: "You are directed to answer the question as to where you were born."

"I was born on November 10, 1904" Reva says. "In Russia, but not in the town the counsel gave."

She had chutzpah. I guess this had been happening for years already and she had seen her friends go through the same process. Anyway, she was prepared to try and face the committee with the government against her, but the constitution was on her side.

Tavenner asks her about the town she was born in and how she became a U.S. citizen. They request names of her family members and her domicile. Then, the committee turns their attention to her work life.

Mr. TAVENNER: "What is your occupation?"

Grandma: "I am a housewife."

Mr. TAVENNER: "Have you held a position of an executive character in any organization?"

Grandma: "Yes, from time to time."

Reva had been blacklisted for at least six years by then, which made it impossible to secure paid work. She lost her job. She lost her home. Despite these facts, it made me smile to read about her self-defining as a housewife with executive leadership experience. *Kick ass.*

Mr. TAVENNER: "Were you the executive secretary of the American Russian Institute?"

Grandma: "Yes."

The American Russian Institute (ARI) was committed to friendship between the Soviet Union and the United States. Not surprisingly, HUAC framed the ARI as a Communist organization and put them on the blacklist. Reva says that she served as the executive secretary of the ARI on and off between 1948 and 1954.

Mr. TAVENNER: "Were you a member of the Communist Party at any time during that period."

Grandma: "I decline to answer that question."

Mr. TAVENNER: "May I ask a question?"

"I decline to answer that question."

Reading the transcript, I can feel her momentum. She is on the defensive and has thought

this through. Tavenner asks her questions about how she was selected for her position. He is trying to get her to mention people's names.

"What do you mean 'designated'" Reva asks. "It's a job like any other job."

The committee asks her a slew of questions about how she was chosen to work at the ARI that she dances around describing her hiring process in general terms. The committee wants names.

Mr. TAVENNER: "Who interviewed you?"

Grandma: "A number of people."

You get the idea. She is trying to stand her ground. Finally, she lets loose.

Grandma: "I will have to decline to answer that question, sir, because I don't believe you have any right to ask me with whom I associate or have associated with. And so I am going to use the first amendment of the Constitution that protects me from that kind of inquiry, and I will also use the privilege and the protection against you asking me questions against my will which is given me under the fifth amendment."

Grandma brings her samovar to staff a booth at the All Nations Festival, Sportsman Park, 1952. Photos courtesy FOIA.

Reva's legal studies were coming in handy after all. She knew her constitutional rights. Tavenner asks her questions about the All Nations Festival on May 18 in 1952 that landed her on page two of the Los Angeles Examiner. She headed a Russian culture booth at the festival and was accused of hanging the Soviet flag. The flag, my father explained to me once, was there before she arrived and after she was hauled away. Tavenner asks if she hung a flag at the festival.

"No, sir; that is incorrect," she says.

Mr. TAVENNER: What occurred then?"

"The Chamber of Commerce arranged booths of all nations which were invited to participate in World Trade Week…We found it there and it remained there when we left."

Tavenner announced that he wants to submit a newspaper article from the Los Angeles Examiner as evidence of irate citizens and Communist propaganda.

Mr. TAVENNER: "Do I understand you disagree with that account of this occurrence?

"I definitely disagree," she says. "Because I think a true picture would have been gotten from the director of the park and from the Chamber of Commerce, rather than the newspapers. And that is the official record."

Mr. TAVENNER: "The institute has been cited, has it not, as Communist by Attorney General Tom Clark?"

Grandma: "Well, there has been such a long list that I, frankly, am not particularly impressed one way or another."

Their debate continues. Tavenner does not like the idea of an exchange of ideas between two countries and is wary of her role in a global dialogue. She defends the organization's mission as aligned with the State Department's new cultural exchange agreement and mentions her enthusiasm for the children's art exhibitions, music, and films they presented. Tavenner questions her about terminology like:

what constitutes an educational panel and what constitutes a public forum? They want to paint her as a rabble-rouser. She sees herself as a cultural bridge between nations. People are often shamed or hurt for acting against corruption, but everyday acts of consciousness can reshape our country and the future.

He returns to his hunt for names to add to his list. She refuses. He asks again and again in different ways. Who spoke? Who paid her? Who did she pay? Who lectured? He mentions people's names, and asks her to confirm their participation in ARI events. She declines each time.

"I am sorry, I will have to decline to answer that question on the same grounds that I have given before, regarding the names of people associated."

Mr. TAVENNER: "Is that because to do so might incriminate you?"

"The question that you posed, of course, is one of my reasons, naturally," she says. "And of course, there is another reason, that I don't want to hurt anyone, and they might very well be hurt by being included as admitted by me in this hearing."

This doesn't stop Tavenner. He prods for names but has no success. He asks her if she is a member of the District Council of the Communist Party.

"Same Question," she says.

He continues to prod.

"Same question, same answer," she says.

Finally, the witness is excused. She leaves the courtroom to speak to journalists outside. I close the file and my eyes. Grandma stood her ground. She was prepared.

My next step is to learn more about the context for the hearing. I read about the Hollywood Ten. I watch *Trumbo*. The stories told about the Cold War make it seem as if it was an ideological battle between white dudes. What about everybody else? Lots of women, immigrants, and ethnic minorities were harassed during the McCarthy era witch-hunts. When I found the documentary *Seeing Red (1983)*, I finally got a better sense of Reva's world. The people in the film are familiar to me, and my grandma's best friend, Dorothy Healey, is in it. I listen to their views, aspirations, and motivations. They are excited to work to improve living conditions for people in their communities. The film also includes redbaiting clips from the 1950s where communists are called "lying, dirty, shrewd, godless, [and] murderous..." One guy from the Federal Bureau of Investigation (FBI) equates Communists with "a malignant way of life akin to disease."

HUAC managed surveillance and interrogated thousands of Americans during the Cold War. [7] The interrogations resulted in public shaming and blacklisting that disrupted their lives significantly, including the ability to find shelter, study, or work. The interrogations were the public climax of years of espionage involving informants, writers, and secret agents who probed into the daily lives of people who were subpoenaed. Reva was subpoenaed and testified in Los Angeles on September 4, 1958. During that year, HUAC interrogated 66 other Angelenos — twenty-nine, about half were women. The list of surnames brought before the committee in Los Angeles includes Jewish, Spanish, Asian, and Anglo surnames from residents of diverse cultural backgrounds. The committee members orchestrating the HUAC interrogations were uniformly white men, predominantly from the South.

How were progressive Jewish women trying to make sense of these times? I welcome Hannah Arendt and Helene Cixous into my living room by reading their work. My home becomes a library. I read Jewish women from the 1950s and 1960s who were writing about exile, migration, statelessness, xenophobia, otherness, Fascism, and the banality of evil. The Jewish diaspora has been nomadic, Cixous reminds me. We are like bromeliads clinging to the walls of the larger nations we inhabit. I wonder how immigrants could ever feel a part of a new nation without being grounded in their own cultural roots. Impossible. Identity doesn't work that way. Culture is cumulative, expanding out from its center. We should be allowed to stay connected to our roots. If not, we may tumble. Reva spent her adult life trying to broker understanding between her place of origin and the United States.

Anyone who knows a thing or two about history knows that bad ideas and despicable behavior can multiply and become the norm. Arendt called this the banality of evil. We must be vigilant so that evil is not normalized. Without communities, refugees remain on the margins: stateless, voiceless, and powerless. Silence equals complicity, Rabbi Prinz said. It is everyone's responsibility to try and see things clearly and defend human rights for all.

I remember a box my dad gave me a few years before he died and seek it out. The flat wooden box appears immediately, as if it was waiting and whistling to me. I find it like a child uncovers the afikoman hidden in a white linen napkin at Pesach. I lift the box from around the tubs of pens, ink, and brushes, and bring it out from hiding. It's made of dark wood, two feet by two feet, about three inches tall. I carry it to the living room and set it on the green ottoman.

I face the box. Unlatch the lid. It springs open. "Old family pictures" is written in my dad's handwriting on a torn piece of paper. Photos from 1934 to 1970 are mashed together inside. The older ones have white jagged borders and my father's notes on their backs. Some are mounted on brown linen, others printed on flimsy paper. Seeing my dad's handwriting is like unearthing a hieroglyphic from inside a cave of prehistoric saber tooth tigers. My eyes tingle. My body feels extraordinary, like an astronaut floating above the Earth in my living room. My own anthropology floats up to greet me.

The photos remind me of the languages that I've lost. I can't decipher the phrases in Russian and Yiddish. Our family lost three languages in two generations: Hebrew, Yiddish, and Russian. Growing up in California, I happily learned Spanish and Portuguese, but these new additions don't replace the ones that I lost. Every language is its own world.

Dad's loop-di-loop cursive notes say: "David's great great grandfather. Amy's great great great grandfather." He must have figured I'd be reading them one day. The box smells of wood, paper, and dust. It's a kind of sarcophagus. The lid is lined with a thin paper print of birds circled by green leaves, pink flowers, indigo clouds, and butterflies. Scrawled on the rice paper is, "1936, Chinese shawl, Gift from Sidney and Reva Finkel, From Havana, Cuba." The box must be from Reva's first marriage, the one that spawned my father.

I look through the photos one at a time and try to organize them in piles: Grandma's early years, the ancients, her first marriage, her work at the ARI. The images are from various nations and cities. My family is connected to more than one people or place.

Time passes imperceptibly. Soon the natural light drains from the room. I am surrounded by my father, grandmother, and the egun.[8] Photos are strewn across my legs, feet, and the couch. I feel like a tattooed woman in the dusk, covered with mixed up moments from a century. No linear time. Scatter. Collision. Mish mash.

Reva is a young woman wearing a boyish tie and knickers. Her short, dark hair is pressed in waves against her head.

My father is a skinny boy sitting on a haystack.

My father floats in a gloomy rowboat with his brother.

He lifts an oar.

Reva is squatting on Venice Beach with a flock of seagulls. Her silver hair drapes down her back. Her skin senses the wind off the shore. The gulls' beaks face into the breeze, but she faces the camera. I read the date printed on the edge. She is fifty-two in this shot. I am fifty-two as her witness.

My father is bent down on one knee offering her a bouquet of wildflowers. She is overacting, pretending to be surprised, one hand over her heart as she brushes her forehead. She smiles like the lucky winner of a million-dollar prize because her children love her.

She is a girl in a wheelbarrow. Why is no one behind her to push?

She is wearing white and playing Ping-Pong under a grove of trees.

She sits on the ground with her children on the chestnut earth. Her arms reach around my dad's shoulders to hold his hands. She appears to be pulling out a splinter from his finger.

She is dressed in a traditional Russian scarf, embroidered white blouse, and skirt. She towers over the camera, looking down. Her left foot is flexed. She looks like she's been singing, and I remember stories of her verses, and how her cousins wore folk costumes and played balalaika in Hollywood movies. This must have been before the Cold War.

She is selling kisses for peace. One hand propped against her hip, and the other balancing a picket sign.

She is glowing in her black dress pinned with a silver floral pendant as she speaks with the Archbishop Red Dean of Canterbury.

She is wearing dark glasses, a black polka dot blouse, and a knee length circle skirt. Her hair is braided in two and wrapped around her head like a bird's nest. Tea brews in the samovar behind her. She leans her arm on a table stacked with books. Posters dangle with drawings of working women and phrases in thick bold type with exclamation points. A woman in an enormous white bonnet concealing her face approaches grandma and leans in menacingly. In a few moments, people will gather around Reva's booth at World Trade Week, and the police will evacuate her body, the tea, and the books from the premises. Black and white photos are taken of the debacle from twenty feet away. Were the shots taken by a spy? The next day, grandma's face, name, and address will be printed on the front page of the newspaper. Headline: "Red Scare."

I have unearthed every image from the box. My hands scrape the wooden bottom. Shards of rice paper clot vacant corners. I stare wide-eyed into the empty box wishing that it could speak for itself. It's a silent face off. I wish my ancestors could spring out talking like those wire bound snakes that leap out of cans for gags. *What should I do now that I've reached the bottom?* No answer. I make a pseudo-mechanical motherly choice. When in doubt, clean. Straighten. Put away. I pick up the box, walk outside, turn it over, bang it three times, knock out the dust, turn it back over, go inside, and set it down. The box, my hands, and the room smell like dust. I taste dust on my lips. I put the photos back in the box. I put the box inside the plastic bag. I put the plastic bag inside the office.

I spend the next few weeks searching the web for more material about her. I'm curious about the informants who followed her around Los Angeles from the 1940s to the 1960s. I don't know much about surveillance except for child's play. When my kids were small, they liked to play with walkie-talkies. They put on dark glasses and ran around the neighborhood pretending to be spies. My daughter says they were inspired by the Latino family in Robert Rodriguez's movie *Spy Kids* who solved mysteries and saved the world from villains. They pretended to be spies in the supermarket when we shopped for groceries. This made me feel more secure because even if I couldn't see them, I always knew that they could see me. It wasn't like that for grandma. Her spies were real. They were everywhere. Dad told me she felt bad for the secret agents and would bring them tea to the car stationed outside her apartment.

Being on the HUAC blacklist was like being cast in a real-as-steel detective movie with secret agents, censored FBI memoranda, and numerical codes assigned to human beings and their topics of conversation. I find a bunch of black and white censored FBI documents from the 1950s with her name on the list of participants and events.

It was sad for me to see her name listed on the FBI documents.[9] It felt invasive, unsettling, and frightening. The typed documents were composed by secret agents, or SAs. There were scarred with lots of empty rectangles and whiteouts on the pages. The forms I could find were liberated for public viewing thanks to FOIA and the American Civil Liberties Union (ACLU). The memoranda begin with the basics: date, location, secret agent name, and list of participants. The lists of human beings included their name, gender, and ethnicity. Sometimes they also included random notes about different people's body types like "She is fat, maybe 45." They have lots of ditto marks, like this:

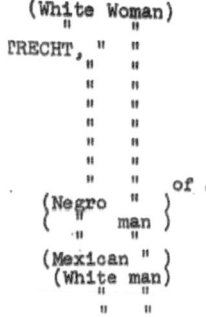

*Example of how FBI informants categorized people
by gender and race in their notes.*

Following the lists and codes, are narrative summaries of what people discussed during the meetings. Reading the FBI reports allowed me to view Grandma and her friends through the lens of the SAs — their words, their writing, and their codes. It's an out of body experience. My heart goes numb. I can't help but wonder which of

Grandma's friends was the informant. How did it feel for her to be constantly under surveillance? How can I believe in a country that would do this kind of thing? Is there a gene that can pass down feeling like an outsider?

This was years after the *Universal Declaration of Human Rights* was passed in 1949. This kind of surveillance should not have been legal. Article 19 says, "Everyone has the right to freedom of opinion and expression"; yet not everyone receives it. This right "includes freedom to hold opinions without interference and to seek, receive and impact information and ideas through any media and regardless of frontiers." [10] I can see the contradiction. Our laws and our practices don't always match. Reading Grandma's surveillance documents make it clear that it isn't always safe in the United States to express one's own opinion. How far have we come since that time, if at all?

I find themes in the SA's notes. There was community-based organizing and grassroots political education going on. There was a progressive intercultural movement brewing in Los Angeles, and Grandma was a part of it. What must have seemed contentious to the SA's is exciting, even inspiring, to me.

Imagining the SAs infiltrating meetings is disturbing. Would you want people listening in on your community meetings pretending to be someone they are not? This scares the crap out of me. It also undermines any hope I may have for democracy and respect for different opinions.

I used to imagine the Cold War as a blip on the historical screen. It wasn't. HUAC was launched in 1938 and the Cold War lasted formally until 1991 with the fall of the Berlin Wall. That's half of the Twentieth Century. The Cold War is as old as me. Let's be real. It's older than me. It's still with us. Just recently, Newt Gingrich said he wanted to resurrect the House Un-American Activities Committee to protect America from Muslims. How can every single person in one of the oldest and largest faiths on the planet be considered dangerous?

Trump's executive order to ban refugees from the United States resembles the stereotyping and attack on immigrants undergirding the Alien Act of 1940. Creating a Muslim registry is akin to a blacklist. Gingrich said that HUAC was created to protect Americans from the Nazis. [11] Well, that's a revisionist history. I don't think that's how it went. Grandma was a Jew, not a Nazi. The Trump administration is once again slandering immigrants and refugees. This stirs up the hysteria that made Grandma's life so hard. Nah. The Cold War didn't crumble with the Berlin Wall. It wants to build a new wall between the U.S. and Mexico in 2017. Cold War ideas are like a zombie that keeps on returning from its grave. It's not dead.

How do spies keep track of everything? Reva's secret agents were numerologists, so let's talk numbers.

First, I was born and raised in 100-1763. That was their code number for Los Angeles.

Second, I'm the granddaughter of 100-26497. That's the number they assigned Reva.

Third, if you discussed racism, Jim Crow laws, or what the FBI called "the Negro Question" and "Negro Matters" in a meeting that was 100-24345.

Fourth, if you wanted to get involved in local governance, circulate a petition, or raise funds for a cause at a community breakfast, the SAs considered that political activity — 00- 23423.

And, fifth (in honor of the fifth amendment) was HUAC. The code for HUAC was 62-1664.

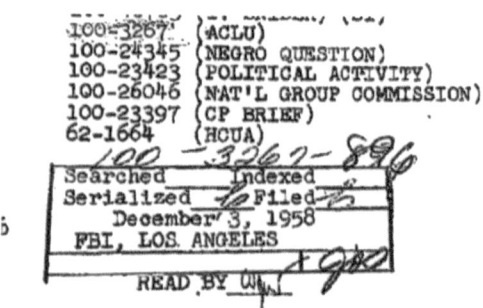

Example of FBI informant categorization of discussion topics including "American Civil Liberties Union" and the "Negro Question."

The SAs were kind of like researchers. They kept field notes and compiled reports. Social scientists call this participant observation. Spies call it espionage. The SAs didn't like petitions. They didn't like community organizing. They didn't like people collaborating across cultures. They didn't like the idea of marginalized people running for local office. SAs took notes about how the community was circulating a petition to denounce HUAC and discussed where to distribute them. A community member is quoted as saying:

> Not only should the Negro churches be a special concentration point, but all other Negro mass organizations should be contacted; and also, Jewish Synagogues, in view of recent bombings of Jewish Synagogues in the South, and the persecution of Jewish people.[12]

I made a list of highlights from the narrative descriptions of community meetings from the SAs:

1) Participants thought that Republicans were making life hard for labor and were

refusing to "support the gains of the Negro people's liberation,"

2) Participants thought that labor needed to become a reliable ally for the civil rights movement,

3) Participants wanted a "complete Labor and Negro Alliance,"

4) Participants felt "an urgency to educate the struggles for alliance of the Communist Party with the Negro people, the Mexican people, and other minority groups."

This is what the FBI was upset about? These are things that must have sounded good to Grandma, and sound appealing to me.

In one report, the SA noted that participants wanted to learn more about the connection between race and class. "Study of the labor question in the Club," an SA reported, "is put off for a couple of weeks until comrades have time to study the James Jackson Statement on the Negro Question." At the following meeting, the SA reports that they "briefly discussed the Jackson report, distributed petitions to Southern California representatives in the Congress of the United States and sold NAACP Christmas seals." [13] I want to sing a song for NAACP Christmas seals. How is distributing NAACP Christmas seals equated with being un-American? Jim Crow absurdity.

Finally, an SA reports that the club was interested in the "minority conference" of the Democratic party and "spelled out the special role and emphasized the strength of the participation of Negro and Mexican aims in political activity...It might even elect Negros, Mexicans, or working-class candidates."

Strangely enough, the SAs taught me something valuable. Grandma and her friends were figuring out how to create solidarities among cultural groups. She was an activist who helped organize across cultures and faiths. Maybe the SAs thought it was a problem for women, immigrants, people of color, and laborers to organize together.

Reva thought that's what democracy was all about. Me, and my poly-lingual, interfaith, intercultural, home are nothing new. I am Reva's apple. She is my tree.

Reading about Reva made me understand why my dad was so in love with the Constitution. He got it from his mom. He believed in the Constitution like Christian kids love

Santa Claus, or babysitters worship Mary Poppins. After completing law school, my dad went to work for the same firm that defended Reva before HUAC (Margolis, McTernan, and Branton). I've been told that the firm was the first unsegregated law firm in the country during the Jim Crow period. Margolis was a Jew. McTernan was white. Branton was black. The firm focused on civil liberties, anti-war cases, and defended people charged as subversives under the Smith Act. I hadn't known that the same firm represented Reva. I learned this from the HUAC proceedings. I hadn't known that the same firm represented my dad, either. Fumbling through a box of handwritten correspondence between my dad and his father (Shloime who was renamed Sidney in Ellis Island) I learned that dad had been stationed at Fort Ord. The firm defended him when he refused to sign the loyalty oath and was accused of having an enduring relationship with his mother, who was accused of being a Communist. Dad argued that one should not have to choose between the tenth commandment and the tenth amendment, between loyalty to family and loyalty to country. Eventually, he won the case and was given an honorable discharge, but not without strain, worry, and a fight. Dad impressed many lessons and values upon me, but he apparently didn't want to share many details from these challenging times. Maybe bad times are best forgotten. If I write about it, will it put my family at risk again to become a target of hatred? Will I write them down in history wrong? If I don't write about it, will important lessons be lost? Is there something to learn from history to help us navigate our struggles today?

I find a typed letter addressed to Reva in the W.E.B. Dubois archive. It was written by Alice Citron, the Secretary of the National Committee to Defend Dr. W.E.B. Dubois and Associates in the Peace Information Center. The letterhead states "Committee to Defend the Advocates of Peace." Written on May 5, 1951, it begins: *"Dear Miss Mucha, Thank you for your reply..."* This surprised me. Before this, I had no idea that Reva was in contact with Dubois' office. The letter is about Dubois' pending visit to Los Angeles. He was touring the country to increase awareness for the peace movement, and to raise funds to defend himself in court against HUAC. His office must have considered Grandma a capable community organizer when they hoped she might organize his event. Dubois was also a friend of Paul Robeson — the actor, singer, and activist. My dad loved to recount the story of being introduced to Robeson by Grandma. He fondly remembered how Robeson's handshake eclipsed his own small hand. This always made him laugh.

Dubois was an expert on the workings of racist capitalism. In 1960, he said:

> Democracy has so disappeared in the United States that there are some subjects that cannot even be discussed. The essence of the democratic process is free discussion. There was a time when men were not allowed to talk about universal suffrage, or the education of women, or freedom for negro slaves. Today, communism is the dirty word. [14]

He knew that the future of peace and justice depended on alliances between fair-minded people of all cultures. HUAC was compromising democracy, not defending it. Hatred squelched our yearning for inclusivity, fairness, and participation.

RED HEARING

Continued from Second Page

housewife, who lives at 5436 Lemon Grove Ave.

She insisted, however, that the American-Russian Institute was not an instrument of the Communist Party or the Soviet government, that it stored no Communist Party literature and that she knew no Russian Communists.

Describes Work

Mrs. Zwolinski described it as a research and lending library which received books, recordings, art exhibits, sheet music and photographs from Russia under the cultural exchange program. She said she was asked about an incident in 1952 when the institute had a Week exhibit at Century Park.

Newspaper accounts at the time said the booth was but down when the hammer and sickle flag was unfurled and literature extolling life under the Communist in Russia was distributed.

Explains Flag

"We were invited by the Los Angeles Chamber of Commerce to have a booth there under the flag of the USSR," Mrs. Zwolinski related. "The booth was there only two hours when the flag was pulled down. We didn't put it up and we did not pull it down."

The subcommittee's policy of holding closed sessions and not discussing the testimony given by witnesses was explained by Chairman Walter thus:

A civil suit brought against the House committee by two of the witnesses subpoenaed, Donald Wheeldin and Admiral George Dawson, has something to do with it.

$20,000 Asked

The suit, charging that the group is an "illegal committee," seeks to quash the subpoenas and asks damages of $20,000 against U.S. Marshal Robert W. Ware and his bonding companies because his men served the subpoenas.

It alleges that being subpoenaed by the committee subjects the men to "public shame, disgrace and ridicule, and falsely stains them with the stamp of disloyalty."

U.S. Judge William C. Mathes dismissed the suit last week but Atty. Wirin is preparing an appeal. Wheeldin failed to appear Tuesday in response to his subpoena and Chairman Walter said he would try to have him cited for contempt.

Called Harassment

"We are convinced the suit is just another method of harassment," Walter said, "but we don't want to make it any easier than possible for them to maintain their suit."

Another reason for the secret sessions, Walter added, is that the committee has not been able to corroborate evidence against some of those subpoenaed.

"We wanted to be abun-

WITNESS — Mrs. Reva Mucha Zwolinski among witnesses at Red hearing.

dantly sure we were not going to injure someone and possibly cause someone to lose his job," he said.

"We wouldn't have a closed hearing for some and an open hearing for others. Rather than take a chance of injuring someone, we decided to have them all closed. This was a decision reached by the full committee in Washington before Congress adjourned."

Walter said that whenever anything is released, it is by action of the full committee.

Purely coincidental to Walter's remarks, there was a case of mistaken identity yesterday. Mrs. Sarah Lord, 1718 Carolina St., San Pedro, showed up completely mystified by her subpoena. Turned out it was another Sarah Lord the committee wanted.

Walter said one of the interesting things developed in the hearing this week is the "terrific struggle" going on in the Communist Party here over some Soviet policies.

"The events in Hungary and the execution of Premier Nagy—which exposed the mailed fist of Russia—made quite an impact," he said.

"It is apparent that Dorothy Healey (southern California chairman of the party) is going to be removed next month."

Mrs. Healey indicated to newsmen yesterday that she is at odds with some in the party because of her disapproval of some Soviet Union policies and may not seek re-election to her post.

Reva reframes describes the independence of her work in the library receiving books, recordings, sheet music, photography, and hosting art exhibits.

After her interrogation, an article was published in the *Los Angeles Times* called "Witnesses Spar at Red Hearing." The layout includes Reva's face in the upper left corner, and she is quoted at length in the piece. She was adamant about not naming names. The article states, "'They had no business asking me,' explained the gray-haired, Russian born housewife who lives at 5436 Lemon Grove Avenue...'" Today, in the digital world, that would be considered doxing, or publishing private information with malicious intent. She had to move. The article also mentions that a civil suit was brought against HUAC for being unconstitutional by a group of Angelenos who were subpoenaed before the committee.

The suit, charging that the group is an 'illegal committee,' seeks to quash the subpoenas and asks damages of $20,000 against U.S. Marshall Robert W. Ware and his bonding companies because his men served the subpoenas. It alleges that being subpoenaed by the committee subjects the men to 'public shame, disgrace, and ridicule, and falsely stains them with a stamp of disloyalty. [15]

Public shame. Disgrace. Ridicule. A false stain. That was the impact of being subpoenaed before HUAC. Despite the shaming, people were fighting back, and Reva was among them. Reva's HUAC hearing was closed to the public. Despite the risk to her personal safety, she spoke with reporters, anyway. Why did she choose to speak? She must have wanted to tell her story to the public in her own words. I feel a similar urge to tell this story now because it shows how history is made through the actions and struggles of everyday people. If our ancestors took risks to fight for inclusion and tolerance, then we can too.

I call my mom and we decide to meet for dinner. She serves us bowls of homemade vegetable soup around the same round table that nourished our family since I was a girl. Me and my mother. The refrigerator and the sink. Two windows and their shades. I relax and tell her that I've been reading up on Grandma Reva.

"I found her HUAC testimony," I say.

"You did?" She raises her spoon in the air. She's interested. I've loosened a string from our family tapestry.

"Yeah, and a bunch of stuff. FBI memoranda. A letter from W.E.B. Dubois' office. A wooden box of old photos. A note from dad about a red scarf."

"Oh. I have that," she says. "It's in my closet."

"The scarf is real?" This clobbered me. I'd found a lot of information online, but not much that I could hold in my hands. The scarf was something palpable I could touch.

"Yes."

Mom leads me down the hallway to her bedroom. She swings open the door to her closet to reveal a row of hanging patterned shirts and pants in blues, blacks, and reds. Colorful necklaces clang against the door as she yanks it open. Her shoes wait obediently in pairs below. A row of boxes is balancing on a surface above us.

"There," she points up. "There it is."

A white hat box is squeezed in between plastic storage containers beyond her reach. I stretch up, jiggle it free, and bring it down. We step away from the closet, holding the hatbox together with our four hands. It is taped shut. Mom starts prying her fingers around the edges of the lid and I secure the bottom. The old, brittle tape splits apart. She wiggles off the lid to expose a cloud of crinkly, cream-colored paper, flecked with small holes. Moths had devoured the paper. Had they destroyed the scarf too? She lifts off the wrapping and we're greeted by a burst of burgundy fabric.

Mom hoists up the enormous maroon shawl embroidered from end to end with light blue chrysanthemums. Blossoms and leaves fill each inch of fabric. The edges are knotted with a foot of thick red thread. The shawl is stunning. Elaborate. Sumptuous. Elegant. It's large enough to conceal a human being. It wants to dance flamenco. It's a cause for celebration. Mom stretches the shawl around her shoulders, and it sweeps the ground. It's a blanket. It's a cape. It's a symphony.

"It's made of silk," she says. "Your grandmother used to spread it across the piano." Mom gathers the fabric in her arms. Warm light streams onto us from a standing lamp. *Where does raw silk comes from? Silkworms? Mulberry leaves? Cocoons.* It's been hiding quietly in a hatbox for half a century. My head shakes in disbelief. It is intact.

"How did you get it?" I say.

"Reva gave it to me," she says, "just like I am giving it to you. Here. Take it." Mom extends her arms and the silk mantón falls into my chest. I feel its weight — thick, sleek silk from the 1800s — the color of blood. The fabric's mint-blue chrysanthemums envelop my arms, wrists, and hands. I'm engulfed in its rich red fabric, flower blossoms and crisp green tendrils. My whole body is smiling. I know that this is what Reva would have wanted me to feel.

Studying my ancestors is a journey that hasn't ended. The more I learn about Reva, the more I admire her tenacity and love of life. She was a revolutionary, an everyday shero. In "Hope and the Historians," Ta-Nehisi Coates (2015) wrote that "the more I studied [history], the more I was confronted by heroic people whose struggles were not successful in their own time, or at all." The Cold War hurt Grandma, but she didn't let the terror of the times stop her from doing what she believed was right. She fought for her vision of a better world, and I can, too. We all can.

Her radicalism was sparked by the pogroms, the Great Depression and the Second World War, and she participated in the progressive social movements of her time. I'd known about her political values, but I didn't know about the intercultural and interdenominational work Grandma and her friends were doing in Los Angeles during the Jim Crow period. I now consider McCarthyism synonymous with Jim Crow and white male supremacy. It's all hate mongering. Same people. Same power structure. Same violence.

We can ask, "who defines America?" The simple answer is that we all do. My Dad taught me that being Jewish means understanding oppression and showing compassion. We can learn from our own histories and from each other. My grandma's story is a tiny light that has helped me find my bearings. This helps me today as we face the revival of xenophobia, racist violence, and misogyny. Even when the Trump Administration shakes me to my core, and I worry about the impact on human rights and the environment, I know that Reva rose to face the times she lived in, and I can, too. I reject ignorance, innocence, and fear. I welcome her courage, resilience, and fascination with beauty and art as my inheritance.

I sit with my daughter Reva at the kitchen table. The mist from our teacups rises into the air. "I need to find a conclusion to the piece about your great grandma," I say. She knows that I've been working on it for a while. She's a writer, too.

"There doesn't need to be a moral to the story," she says. "The point is, she worked for future generations the same way that we are working for future generations."

I swear I didn't make that up. I couldn't have. I just listen and write it down.

Author's maternal grandmother Frida Raschke with her siblings, parents, and grandfather. Above (L - R): Velv, Tsipora, Frida. Below (L - R): Tama Ester, Alter Shloime Noach, Avram Duvid.

The ancestors are rounding our diasporic family up. Gathering us back into rows of seats. Dressed in thick black cotton. Only our hands and faces are naked to the air. We pause before a contraption made of metal and glass. A small mirror inside the device can capture stillness.

My pe'ot, long as centipedes, are tucked into each side of my cap. Oh, to be still and wait. Recorded in a moment that is not my own. My white beard and mustache fan open above my lungs. I breathe. My hands are delicate and paddled like a marine mammal. My jacket crosses the center of my belly and is held in place by one round button. I am thinner than my clothes. My eyes, hallowed in their sockets, have seen so much. Too much. My mouth of flaming-white-lions sips silence. My fingers rest together. Apart from them, fan out the thumbs. My hands were schooled by touching pages of the Talmud.

My son's hands are wide. They labor with wood. Six buttons crisscross the center of his long jacket. He built the boat for our survival and our loss. His hands discipline offspring. He will sit shiva for his disobeyers before they perish. He annihilates desire with orthodoxies.

My granddaughter is not convinced. Her hand doubles into a small fist on his shoulder. She stands behind us, balancing on her own feet in her natural hair. Her eyes are like my eyes, hollowed by the same deep curves. She wishes.

I ponder, holding what cannot be said. I chose locusts and sunshine. Anything, but to be a Jew in Europe. Every day I doven. I pointed us toward the Mediterranean, wrapping black strips of leather around my wrist and forehead.

We wandered beyond the trepid fate of our communities. We will forget Warsaw, Przasnysz, Jablonka. There is no reason to remember or return. Kalisz will be remembered only by a handwritten K in the corner of a Torah that calendars our time. Births charted in handwriting in the margins. Spine split open from wear.

I sit at the center of my small fortification. Our band of humans who escaped history. We planted our legs and arms in the sand, lifted up skirts and the hems of pants. Our legs became thick as palm trees.

My daughter-in-law is ceramic black eyes. Dark wig. Un-inflatable mouth. Her hands are folded like parchment on her lap. Someday, she will come to be our first citizen. She will be able to speak at least one of the formal languages of now. The British will mandate her in Palestine where we will live forever, until forever has gone. She will sleep in the living room beside two sets of grandchildren dreaming head to foot on trundle beds.

We will lose a granddaughter to a non-believer and then suicide. We will lose a grandson to a mustache, vest, and tie.

My hands were soft to the pages. I dwelled in the everyday breath of ritual. My days and nights observe the halacha that kept us alive through calamitous, nascent times.

One day, two of my unknowns — my great, great, great granddaughters — will call out Saba Raba Raba! They will walk into the dusk where I am buried, wade through the night, past tall tree silhouettes, beside the shoulder-orchestra of the departed. They will read me where I rest and see my memory rectangle. I deliver them a wild green plant that broke through concrete. A gift that is able to grow anywhere — maybe even everywhere.

Change of Name Notified in Palestinian Gazette No. 5/9589

My name is Tema Ester.

My name is Avram Duvid, Abrama Dawida Szlas.

My name is Bruria Shimshon.

My name is B.

My name is A.

I am named after my grandmother's grandmother.

I am the son of Alter Shloime Noach, grandson of Velvl.

A wolf is born in every generation.

My name must speak one of the official languages.

My name does not speak the official languages.

My name speaks some of the official languages.

My name must transmute languages.

My birth date is 1873.

My birth date is 1869.

My birth date is August 2, 1932.

No one knew when they were born.

On December 4, 1940, I am deceased.

On December 4, 1940, I am 67.

On December 4, 1940, I am 8.

I will be born on December 4.

The applicant for naturalization died.

I have been stateless for 28 years.

I was born in Jablonka.

I was born in Przasnysz.

I was born in Jerusalem in the Bukharan quarter.

I follow behind camels & goats.

I sleep beside Safta, head to tail like fish.

My profession is a carpenter.

My profession is a bricklayer.

My profession is a homemaker.

My profession is an artist.

I am married.

I am a widow.

I am asleep.

I sleep on the floor by the ice box.

Family Mizrah made by Israel Dov Rosenbaum in Pitkamien .
The date on the artwork is 1877.

Facing East

What would you give your child if you knew you might never see them again? Israel Dov Rosenbaum, my paternal great-great-grandfather, gave his daughter Bessie papercut artworks he made by hand. They are now considered to be among the greatest surviving examples of Jewish paper cutting. Art is a vessel for our knowledge, values, and cultures. It can also be a gift of love that connects the generations. One of the papercuts was a מִזְרָח (mizrah), designed to orient Bessie East, toward Jerusalem, from wherever she landed in the diaspora. Another was an amulet for expectant mothers to protect their descendants. Since Israel's Hebrew name contained the letters of one of the names of God, he reshaped the lines of a ל (*lamed*) into a א-ל (*lamed-aleph*) in his signature to protect its sanctity. Six generations later, these gifts to his daughter continue to inspire new stories.

Israel Dov Rosenbaum (L) with Herman (C) and Shloime / Sidney (R).
Photograph taken in Brody, Austro-Hungarian Empire at the turn of the century.

It would be impossible for me to tell you a complex, 150-year-old story in a few words. But I can tell you a tale about art, culture, and family. The papercuts of my great-great-grandfather Israel Dov Rosenbaum reveal the power of art and culture to ground us in history, create spaces for community connection, and imagine brighter futures.

This story points to distinct aspects of my family tree. I think about culture in terms of seven generations. My heritage is 100% Jewish, and our family's futures are Jewish, Black, and Latine. My children's pasts are also African descended from a forced migration to Brazil. This means that I hold love and respect for all aspects of our family tree past, present, and future. My ancestors fled fascism in Europe. No one who remained survived. My father was born in New Jersey, and my mother was born in Jew in Palestine under the British mandate. My children's father is from Salvador da Bahia, the Black Mecca of Brazil. Our family lives in the United States, Israel, Canada, Uruguay, and Brazil. This story provides a narrative that affirms possibilities for Jewish and Black love, and ethical approaches to immigration, inclusion, and art. I would like to think that Israel Dov had his hand in this somehow, albeit as an ancestor.

In December 2022, my mother Bruria (a fine artist in her own right) received a box of old calendars and address books produced by the Jewish Museum in New York emblazoned with Israel Dov's mizrah. The box also contained a copy of the original gift agreement arranged by his grandson Sidney with his second wife Helen Finkel. What should Mom do with the box?

"Throw it away," my brother said.

"Give it to Amy," she decided.

We rummaged through it together. I searched online in the Jewish Museum's collection for his artwork with the aim of requesting copies for the family. Then, quite unexpectedly, a URL popped up. Israel Dov's artwork was somehow linked with the esteemed portrait artist Kehinde Wiley. *Huh? What does my great-great-grandfather have to do with Kehinde Wiley?*

Unbeknownst to my family, Wiley had chosen Israel Dov's mizrah as an immersive background for a portrait in his series *The World Stage: Israel.* He had repainted Israel Dov's iconography and had centered within it a handsome portrait of a young, Jewish Israeli man of Ethiopian descent, Alios Itzhak. When I saw our family mizrah (1877) beside the Alios Itzhak portrait (2011) it struck me in a profound way that ignited mixed emotions and the desire to learn more.

I felt proud to see that Israel Dov's work was being honored. I also felt a sense of loss when I noticed his signature covered over by the portrait. I wanted him to be remembered, not erased. We had grown up admiring Israel Dov's paper cuts on the eastern walls of our homes. I missed his amazing images of tree branches and curling text, and a temple guarded by unicorns, fish, and oxen in colorful geometrical shapes. His work was a reminder that we come from something beautiful, not only from painful stories of war or genocide. At the same time, it was comforting to know that the Jewish Museum is able to care for them properly as fragile objects.

The new portrait is gorgeous. Wiley's series speaks to my family in myriad ways including my father's lineage, my mother's birthplace in Jerusalem, and as a family who descend from Jewish and African diasporas. Seeing Black and Jewish imagery together in Wiley's work filled an important need for me. As a young woman, I was once told by a religious elder that Jewish culture is maintained through the family and that marrying someone who is not Jewish would constitute the death of my culture.

"You can't do that," he said.

A quick glance at my DNA reveals that this idea prevailed throughout my family history. On the 23andMe App, I'm all aqua — 100% Jewish, while my children's father is a rainbow of geographies,

85% of which are Sub-Saharan African. We raised our kids with the belief that being a family of different heritages inspires the opportunity to learn and know twice as much: 200% not half. This means honoring our global connections, and practicing the best qualities of Jewishness, Candomble, and Ifa. The language of Ifa is Yoruba. Kehinde means twin, or ibeji. My mother's first language was Hebrew. In my poem "sidur / a new book could be written," I make this wish: "may the bloody generations of outsidering end with us." It is exhilarating to see how Wiley's work connects my great-great-grandfather's vision of beauty and belonging with anti-racist values and affirmation of Blackness. Wiley's *The World Stage: Israel* centers multiple expressions of Jewishness, Blackness, and masculinity.

When I told my family about Wiley's portrait within Israel Dov's mizrah, we all got to talking. How had we become separated from the mizrah itself? How had the mizrah's story continued to evolve? I even posted on social media about my surprise and my friends gawked in disbelief. A friend of my daughter had studied the mizrah and didn't even know it was made by one of her best friend's ancestors. This inspired a conversation with my son about spiritual objects and their appearances in contemporary art. He practices both Ifa and Judaism but felt that the mizrah "should not have a person on it."

Many social forces separate families from their stories and their heritage. Assimilation, colonization, and genocide forge barriers that make it difficult to know one's origins, communicate with parents and grandparents, or read our ancient texts. We can sustain our mother tongues. Rosenbaum's papercuts and Wiley's portraits remind us we need not be defined by trauma. We are also defined by beauty and restoration.

In my family, my grandfather playfully called himself "Shloime from Podkamien." Shloime Rosenbaum was renamed Sidney Finkel in the United States, and his Yiddish was replaced by English. A similar dynamic occurs when Ethiopian Jews in Israel are asked to rename themselves or supplant Amharic with monolingual Hebrew. The price of inclusion should not mean the loss of culture, language, and our unique differences. Instead, I welcome polylingualism to enjoy cultural continuity. We can speak as many languages as we wish.

Culture, ritual, and art are tools for teaching and learning. I see Israel Dov Rosenbaum paper cuts as his way of connecting our community to a sense of place through his mizrah, and manifesting positive futures through his amulet for expectant mothers. Similarly, Kehinde Wiley's portrait of Alios Yitzhak honors Jewish African heritage and imagines new futures through art.

The paper cuts and painting have been diligently analyzed by art historians in the book that accompanied the exhibition of Wiley's *The World Stage: Israel* in 2011. As a living contemporary painter, there are opportunities to learn more about Kehinde Wiley's life and work. Little has been known about Israel Dov Rosenbaum, and I can fill in some basic information from the family. He lived in the shtetl of Podkamien in the 1800s when the shtetl was a part of the Austro-Hungarian Empire His daughter Bessie fled Europe in the late 1800s for the United States. Israel Dov and his wife, whose name we do not know, raised my grandfather Shloime until Bessie was able to send for him. This took nine years. He was her child from a levirate marriage. She fled Europe to escape Aryan supremacy and fascism, and, most likely, a forced marriage. In New Jersey, she co-created a new family with a partner of her choice named Bernard Finkel. She was involved in the Sisterhood of Temple B'nai Abraham led by Rabbi Joachim Prinz who spoke at the March on Washington. My father was one of Sidney's two sons, George and David, both children from his first marriage to Reva Mucha who emigrated to the United States from Kherson.

I was very curious about how Israel Dov's work came to be used in Kehinde Wiley's painting. I emailed the Jewish Museum and spoke with their curatorial staff. They immediately added the names of living relatives to the object metadata, and, a few months later, they invited me to write this post from a family perspective.

Meanwhile, Kehinde Wiley had an opening of new works in Los Angeles where I live. I went with the hope of meeting him. The line to get in snaked around the block. Inside, I noticed the book *The World Stage: Israel* and was able to flip through its pages. Israel Dov's iconography was wrapped inside the cover, and featured in the opening essay, "Yearning for Jerusalem." The essay discusses the mizrah from an art historical perspective. The book cited my great-great-grandfather's name, the year it was completed, and the place Podkamien. Missing were any details of the person who made the work, or how it came to be in the Jewish Museum collection.

The gallery opening was loud, festive, and boisterous. I pushed through the crowd and found Wiley beside an enormous painting posing for photographs. I waited in line, and when it was my turn, I congratulated him and asked if I could quickly share a strange story. I opened the book, pointed to the page, and said, "This is my great-great-grandfather."

He titled his head to one side, "Excuse me?"

I felt like a ghost, a living emissary of a dead object in a catalog. Here stands a descendant of an image that you have painted. My body became a reminder that artworks are made by people. I touched my index finger to the page and spoke our names aloud: "Israel Dov Rosenbaum, Shloime Rosenbaum (Sidney Finkel), David Finkel (my father), me. Israel Dov Rosenbaum is my great-great-grandfather."

He got the message and pulled me in close for a hug.

"We must honor this somehow!" Wiley said, reaching out a long arm to his studio manager.

"I don't believe that my great-great-grandfather would have ever imagined that this would have happened with his mizrah," I said. "I also don't believe that he could have imagined that his great-great-great-grandchildren would be both Jewish and Black."

The sounds, bodies, and colors of the crowded party swirled around us, but I felt at peace inside. I had tried to do the right thing for my ancestors' memory. Israel Dov Rosenbaum's artwork has taken an unimaginable journey from a rural shtetl to an urban megalopolis, from a home space to prominent museums and galleries. His imagination traveled by foot, horse, train, and boat from Podkamien through Hamburg to New York, California, and Jerusalem.

"Your great-great-grandfather was an artist?!" someone asked me at Wiley's opening.

I never got to meet Israel Dov Rosenbaum, but I did know his grandson, my grandfather Sidney. My thoughts circled back to our kitchen table where I once interviewed him with my father David. This gave me a sense of what life was like for children in Podkamien.

"Jews didn't get to go to school," he stated matter-of-factly. He wanted me to never take access to public education for granted. I also learned from him about gender segregation. The boys went to the Rabbi's house to study Torah and the girls would stay home and do chores.

"Lunch was a crust of bread," he said. "Sometimes we would rub a clove of garlic on it for flavor."

I removed my hands from my pockets and looked up. *Artist.* Of course, my great-great-grandfather was an artist, but I don't know if he would have referred to himself that way. He created beauty for his family and community's spiritual sustenance. His art came from a completely different context from this pristine, white-walled gallery we were standing in on La Brea Boulevard in Los Angeles. The arts flow through my family without end. My mother is a fine artist. I am a poet and dancer, my son is a composer, and my daughter is a filmmaker.

"Yes," I said. "He was an artist, but in a very different time and place."

Family photo in Los Angeles (L-R Reva, Avila, and Amy.)

The Rosenbaum mizrah now links six generations to an ancient and evolving story of identity, family, and community. Two works of art—Israel Dov Rosenbaum's mizrah and Kehinde Wiley's *Alios Itzhak*—now exist in eternal relationship.

We pushed open the gallery doors. Outside, the brisk night engulfed our bodies. I filled my lungs with air.

Turns out, my friend had videoed the hug. I shared it in a group text with my family.

"Aṣẹ oo" my son Avila wrote back, blessing our encounter in the Yoruba language of one of his faiths.

"So, he was nice?" my brother Adam texted.

"Yes," I bubbled back.

"Well, he's a part of the family now," my mother Bruria said. "That is the pleasure."

Then Israel Dov Rosenbaum's great-great-great-granddaughter, my daughter Reva, chimed in.

"That is beautiful."

CONVERSATIONS

Writing Can be a Freedom Vessel

An Interview with Nosakhare Collins (Nigeria)

Nosakhare Collins (NC): Hello, Amy. We are beyond pleased to have you join us.

Amy Shimshon-Santo (AS²):
Thank you for inviting me. It is a joy to be together.

NC: Can you talk about the ways in which your own cultural background has influenced your use of language and the way you teach?

AS²: My cultural background has been shaped by migration, history, and place. I was born on the unsucceeded land of the Tongva and Chumash, in the region of Aztlan (a Nahuatl word for the place of herons). This territory was colonized by Spain, Mexico, and the United States. Located in the Pacific Rim, we are territorially, culturally, and linguistically connected to the Americas (North America, Central America, and South America) and to Oceania and Asia via the Pacific Ocean. African presence has been recorded here since at least the 18th century (half of the LA founders were Black, half were Native American, and two were Spanish). Today, the African diaspora is around 9 % of the population, and one third is foreign born. LA is now a mosaic of communities who speak around 200 different languages at home.

My mother was born in Jerusalem, and my father was born in Newark. Our ancestors fled Aryan nazism, or were annihilated. Raised in LA, I had children with an Afro-Brazilian person of the Candomble faith (an offshoot of the Yoruba Ifa tradition). We made a polylingual, interfaith, multinational family. My Egun, or ancestors, are Jewish. We've been nomadic for over 1000 years. Our languages include Hebrew, Aramaic, Yiddish, Ladino, and the host languages of every place that we have lived. In our tradition, the Hebrew letters speak directly to the divine and are spiritual tools for world making. Polylingualism and translation help my family and friends stay connected across continents. As an artist, I play with how to bring these qualities onto the page and into performance. As a professor, I strive to create inclusive classroom ecologies so that students can be themselves, innovate in their research and artmaking, and study truth from multiple perspectives.

NC: In your experience as an educator, what are some of the most effective ways to help students develop an appreciation for writing?

AS²: Start by establishing a devoted relationship with your own creativity. Tell yourself, *I will show up for you. I will listen to you. I have faith in you. My creativity is limitless.*

There is a lot of strain on us to care for the material needs of ourselves and families. If you come from a working-class family, poetry might appear frivolous. But writing is a way to change our worlds. Welcome writing and reading into your daily life, your routines, your home, your relationships, your dream life, your imagination. Create rituals that satisfy your curiosity, so you don't become stagnant or defeated. Bring poetry into the spaces that you touch. Advocate and organize for book sharing, digital access, music, dance, and media making. Develop ways for communities to connect, perform, and publish. Grow mutualist friendships and leverage your collective resources to expand what is currently possible. Your voice and powers of communication are infinite and are of tremendous value to the world.

NC: What do you hope readers and audiences experience when they encounter or interrogate your work?

AS²: I hope that they feel. I hope that they feel less alone. They may realize that women are dynamic human beings with complex inner and social lives. We are culture makers, not just reproducers of humanity. I come from a lineage where women did not have many opportunities to speak about their lives publicly through writing. No one I am aware of in my lineage wrote. Women have been positioned as the yud — the smallest letter of the aleph bet. (The yud looks like this: ') We are not inconsequential. I hope that readers feel invited into the worlds that I inhabit and feel inspired to write their own stories.

NC: How important is research to you when writing, and in what specific instances has it been a defining factor?

AS²: The first and last person who I must teach is myself. Research lets me move forward and backward in time across space. It lets me learn from the living and the dead, from people I have never met, and from the natural environment. It helps me touch things beyond my reach. I enjoy diving into archives and libraries. I like listening to people; talking with people. A big part of research is filling in the gaps where hegemony has erased or misrepresented so many of us. Performing research has pushed me to think for myself, center my own values, create new terminologies, and shift the narrative of hegemony. Rather than spending my life feeling disempowered or alienated, the trick has been to bring myself, my communities, and the ideas I care about, center stage on the page. Thinking and feeling better seeds different futures in this very moment.

NC: From your perspective, how do you think writing can be used as a means of exploring and expressing issues related to social justice, empathy, and inclusivity?

AS[2]: Anything can be a tool for justice. A dinner shared. An ethical work environment. A safe place to sleep. Better legislation. Kindness. So can writing. Writing is a way to rehearse freedom of speech, practice self-authorship and truth telling, and think critically while cultivating empathy, authenticity, and courage. Through unique language, we can challenge the respectability of how things are to be told. Everything expansive starts as something small. Change could begin with your mark on the page, your voice speaking up. We cultivate empathy and the ability to listen or be heard. We reimagine our lives through language. Our words are how worlds are made.

NC: In your opinion, how do you think educators can help immigrant students develop their voice as writers, without altering the unique writing style and cultural perspective of the students?

AS[2]: Let me begin with a word for students. Value yourself and your dreams. Find trustworthy friends and mentors. Put your leadership traits to work. Advocate for what you want and hope for. You may need to create spaces for support that don't already exist. This could be as simple as a study group, a student run or community press, or a fundraising campaign. Find ways to create a culture of connection, whether on campus, in the community, or online. Your health and wellness is the foundation of your future success. So, rest. Get fresh air. Nourish yourself. No matter how busy you become, you get to set boundaries, say no, and create safe spaces for yourself.

I'm not convinced that students enjoy their education. That is crazy to me. As an educator, I put a lot of effort into developing an inclusive curriculum. I also like to meet with students individually early on to get a better sense of who they are. My aim is for each student to see their cultures reflected in the curriculum. Most of us are denied this. I was denied this. This is something I've focused on changing by making my classes student-centered. The class flow and assignments can provide ways for students to practice self-leadership and responsibility, make creative choices, and practice ethical collaboration. I often require students to connect with people and places outside of school. This helps us be attentive to both academic methodologies and real-world conditions and everyday knowledges.

NC: You are an accomplished writer and educator. What is the biggest difference you have noticed between both worlds and how do you navigate it?

AS[2]: Both teaching and writing begin with the solitary process of research. Teaching quickly becomes an extroverted activity. Teaching worlds vary depending on the context. In the community, we could be anywhere from a park to a community center, or a kitchen table. In the neoliberal university, there are numerous institutional requirements. I've directed two university programs, taught in higher education for 20 years. Universities are highly structured worlds. On the scale of the classroom, my job is to fabricate our starship, take students on a quick spin around the galaxy, and let them take charge of our journey. Writing poetry is a more personal and vulnerable world. It exists less in my head, and more in my body. Even though I love both, I can't always easily switch from one to the other. This quandary is not as simple as time management. It requires navigating different aspects of your own being.

NC: How do you see the role of technology in education, particularly in terms of promoting linguistic and cultural diversity?

AS²: To begin with, I view traditional art and cultural forms — such as dance, music, song, poetry, fashion, and textiles — as technologies, or techne (making and doing). New technologies have made it possible to teach online, and to facilitate learning spaces between people in rural and urban spaces across regions and countries. This absolutely lends itself to cultural, economic, and linguistic diversity. For example, I recently hosted an online class for people across three time zones with participants from various cities in the U.S., Mexico, Ghana, and Nigeria. I'd love to do more of that, but in person. I fantasize about hosting arts and culture residency experiences internationally where we can meet, create, and collaborate face-to-face. We need to be able to experience what is just outside the device or zoom box. Technology has also helped access for students who benefit from audio, transcription, or translation services. Becoming familiar with audio, video, and web technologies is helpful for publishing, and for circulating orality and indigenous languages across time and place.

At the same time, it is also important not to romanticize technology. The inequities of our analogue worlds followed us into our digital worlds. We can remain critical and vigilant regarding the ethics and impact of tech. The internet was influenced by military intentions, and social media was structured around advertising and sales. In the U.S. context, this has created new addictions and mental health concerns associated with a loneliness epidemic. There are new risks associated with AI, and selling people's personal data has become an obstacle to basic democratic systems like voting. The same vigilance and commitment to justice we have in analogue spaces is required with new technologies.

Bodies, Genders, and Authoring the Feminine

Interview with Ana Rita Santiago and Tatiana Pequeno
(Brazil)

A+T: What highlights can you share with us regarding the possibilities and constructions, but also the contradictions and silencing faced in professional academic practice?

AS[2]: The possibilities for teaching and learning through literature are endless. But languages and letters also maintain systems and circuits of power. We become accustomed to limits, barriers, and violence. We navigate the everyday struggles of survival. We know what it's like to be excluded, violated, or invisible. So, the author meditates on what she wants to create and how to shape her imagination into a tangible form. We cultivate abundant, strong, ethical, boundless imaginations.

In every academic leadership position I've held, I have tried to open up inclusive spaces in the classroom and bridge the gap between the university and communities. It is critical to value distinct types of knowledge and learn to dream together. Our personal dreams can be woven into shared dreams. We face silencing by opening our mouths, listening well, and releasing our stories into the world with creativity, commitment, and devotion.

A+T: Tell us a little about your paths as a writer, with bodies, genders and sexualities as crossings and centralities?

AS²: When I entered primary school, being a student felt like a process of disciplining the body and the head. I realized that studying required a certain sacrifice of my culture and personality.

I became an artist early on. I always felt confident in the creative process. I write to exist and to create alternatives and futures. I have already participated in many actions of social, cultural, and educational change. Writing has had the ability to bring about a change within me. This is important for society.

My first published poem was an erotic poem. It was explicit, non-violent, and intentionally non-heteronormative. It caused quite a stir. "I read your poem!" women would say to me as I passed through town, as if I had only written *one*.

At that time, I was working as the director of a graduate program in cultural management. I was afraid of people seeing me as a human person, as a woman in body and soul. Yes, it caused a scandal. My world shook but did not fall.

Many years later I participated in two literary festivals in West Africa. A poetry performance was scheduled in front of a luxurious foreign embassy. The police were not friendly to the writers entering the space. Poetry does not accept policing. Each poem has its own medicine, and I was looking for the right medicine for that moment. I considered reading a poem about police brutality or the persistence of colonial rule. I have many in that vein. Instead, I chose to read the erotic poem to a crowd in front of the police outside the embassy. It was a good scandal. I learned that the body has its own strength, and a poem can shift the politics of space.

A+T: What are some of your strategies of resistance and your intellectual thinking about literature?

AS[2]: During my own process of mental decolonization, I have asked myself what is literature? As a dancer and capoeirista, I consider movement as language, and choreography and body improvisation as publication on the body. I have colleagues who consider images and textiles forms of literature.

My literary friendships with Gloria Carrera, Teio Xaggat, Delia Xochitl Chavez in Mexico, Sabata Mpho-Sokae in South Africa, Mamle Wolo and Abena Awuku Larbi in Ghana guided me towards plurilingualism and indigeneity as a literary path. They inspired me to learn more about my roots and mother tongues. Reading *Decolonizing the Mind*, written by Thiong'o Wa Ngugi, confirmed this path. I began to see languages as operating systems that moderate our social relationships and the circulation of knowledge.

Wherever you go, the land always speaks more than one language. Colonization has alienated us from languages, cultures, and worlds. I started to emphasize plurilingualism, translocalism, and valuing mother tongues in relation to each other and to international languages. This raised numerous issues of lexicon, technology, and communications. We can honor ancestors and cultivate educational and literary futures that value multiplicity within and among us. Walt Whitman wrote, "I contain multitudes." Gwendolyn Brooks wrote, "we are each other's harvest ... / we are each other's magnitude and bond."

A+T: From your personal experience as a teacher, writer, and intellectual, how do you analyze the relationship between female authorship of literature in relation to bodies, genders and sexualities?

AS²: I start with my personal, family, and community experiences. The word has power. When I started teaching in the university, I wanted my students to feel more confident about writing their stories in an authentic and original way. I taught that "writing well" meant being honest. Write honestly, and the outcome will be good. Embracing self-authorship and authenticity are key to creating and transforming spaces.

A+T: Is it possible to write beyond some formulas and themes that are still urgent, but worn out, such as "resistance"?

AS²: Absolutely. The world is always changing. Every word that exists arises from a historical-geographical context. Meanings also change just like contexts sway, quake, and change. We need to have the creativity and courage to name our current experiences. Words are intellectual heritage, but we have the right (and the opportunity) to name what needs to be said right now in a way that is satisfying.

A+T: What are your concerns as a writer and teacher at this moment in terms of female authored literature? What moves you in these times to think and forge new writing projects?

AS²: The writings of intersectional women are broad, expansive, and necessary. The study of local languages, translation, connecting authors, and access to publication, can advance the great possibility that is translocal female authorship. We need to cultivate cultural ecologies—from basic literacies in schooling to community-based lifelong learning, and from publishing to the distribution and circulation of ideas and knowledge objects. Patriarchy and racial capitalism have deformed education and literature. Our opportunity is to remake them in everyone's image. That begins with the act of self-authorship to assert authority over erasure or misrepresentation.

A+T: What do you want as a writer, in terms of achievements and expressions?

AS²: I want us to take our words, relations, and knowledge seriously so that we can author better lives and futures. I want to cultivate spaces of connection and mutuality that are translocal and polylingual. I want to cultivate cultures capable of caring for the planet in this time of climate crisis. And I want to thank all the good people who have inspired and conspired with me along the way.

Pep Talk for Culture Makers

I end this book with a pep talk and pitch for the power of storytelling. There are myriad ways to create change over time, and the stories of working together are ripe for the telling. Storytelling can create public memories of lives in action. Shaping public memory can inspire new improvisations and fresh approaches to living. I hope that you have read this book with the aim of repurposing and composting knowledge for your own ends. My life is one microscopic flash in galactic time. As long as this heart keeps thumping I'll be culture making — one experience at a time. Call this piecework.

As a small elder, I've learned that the next generation is observing how we are with each other and how we treat ourselves —even when we believe no one is noticing.

"We are a river," I once said to my friend Àkpà.

"We are a river," he echoed, "and you are flowing into us."

He made the sentence better. We are a river. We are flowing into each other. Being a part of a river acknowledges how our elders and ancestors poured into us, and how we can pour into each other, flowing toward futures that deserve the very best from us.

During the pandemic, novelist and physicist Martin Egblewogbe asked me to give a pep talk for young writers in the Writers' Project Ghana's (WPG) Mo Issa mentorship program where I'd been serving as a poetry mentor. As a mother and educator, I give informal pep talks all the time, but I'd never delivered one intentionally as a speech. Pep talks aim to convey courage and enthusiasm through motivating language. They must transmit epistemic confidence. It's a challenging time right now to convey confidence. We are experiencing and witnessing suffering and abuses of power near and far. But, we can be confident in our values. Confident in the commitment to practice good character. Confident that the rivers of change will keep flowing in unexpected ways.

The best momentum for change is enthusiasm. After I delivered the pep talk, a vital conversation blossomed in the chat.

A young writer named Atta Atta Brown wrote: "we have stories to tell and we can't sleep."

Well, that's a fantastic reason to write. It is plenty.

The chat conversation veered toward the challenges of making art and making a living. How will we make art and culture while living well in the material world? This dilemma is a sticking point. We all must eat. We all need a place to live. I have had to labor in multiple ways. I've cleaned bathrooms, swept streets, soldered velcro wallets, sold sandwiches, taught capoeira, choreographed dances, and been a professor. I've even left jobs that put my health at risk, or compromised my integrity, even when I needed the money for our basic needs. Without romanticizing creativity, I've noticed that being an artist continues to restore my sense of value, wonder, and worth. I have always needed to make a living, but I have also needed to dance and to write. Maybe that's true for you too.

In the chat, we writers theorized the emptiness of the stomach, the need to write, the demands of publishing, and the inevitability of our demise. Someone compared the discussion to a "showmanship of gladiators fighting with wooden swords," who "each went home in full skin." In our arguments, writers cited Plato, Hippocrates, Conan, Shakespeare, Bukowski, Solomon, Nietzsche, Darwin, the church, philology, nihilism, and idealism to defend their perspectives on art and commerce. All in good fun. It was frolicking nerdom.

When we cite people, we gather their ideas around us for support. We cite to include ourselves within a larger community of ideas —we blanket ourselves with other people. When I scrolled back through the chat, I noticed that not one woman philosopher, educator, or thinker had been cited. The word "woman" was only mentioned as a body vessel for miscarriage or potential cancer. Prince was the only Black artist cited, and no writer from Latin America, Asia, or any indigenous group worldwide had been cited. Nobody's mother, auntie, or neighbor was invoked. The literatures cited to gain authority in this chat were uniformly men, and 99% white. And there were no white men among us. This is what a colonial education has done to us, has done to our play, our intellectuality, and our imaginations. It has done this everywhere.

Most people in the world have been written out of the archive. And, as a result, el mundo no se conoce. The world doesn't know itself. Certainly, we do not know each other on our own terms. Restoration, communication, and imagination are imperative for liberation of any kind. We can endeavor to write the wisdom and strategies of our peoples and places. We can write and read across genres. Write and read in all of our languages. Read and listen to worlds near and far.

If we write our lives, and read more broadly, maybe our stories will weave together a makeshift planetary consciousness and create cultures that reject erasure or denigration. In *The Myth of Normal,* physician Gabor Maté writes that "this is a socio-political moment that is typified by the spread of negativity, distrust, hostility, and polarization…Something is amiss in our culture itself." Taking care of one's health is the start, but, as Maté suggests, "our concept of well-being must move from the individual to the global."

I'm infatuated with the possibility of cultivating planetary consciousness. Everything from bees to trees are awake and share knowledge. Human consciousness is distinguished by the ability to time travel in our thoughts, and share common intentions. Despite our qualia, or uniqueness, we are all made of the same cosmic stardust. Lacking consciousness signifies ignorance, unkindness, or confusion.

Unconsciousness means being asleep, comatose, or even dead. The word consciousness is an impressive accumulation of letters: two c's, o's, and n's, four s's. One I. At the most basic level, being conscious points to the "I," the self.

Humans turn to stories —whether spoken, written, sung, danced, stitched, or painted— to make sense of our lives, face our histories, and build futures. Imagine yourself in the storyteller's shoes, perhaps going someplace you've never been. Then return home to yourself with a wider lens on what it means to be alive.

Writing your stories is infinitely useful. If someone dies, you can write an obituary. Fall in love, and you can write love letters. If someone is mistreated, write a complaint. If the mass media omits your news, blog about it. Not only can we write, but we can speak, edit, publish, teach, and encourage other people to write too. We can write essays and poems and books, curate events and teach and learn, run spaces and influence governance. We can use our creativity to make culture, make change, and make friends.

Dear Reader, I hope that you write so the world can read you. Imagine that your words are weather. Imagine them, rainmakers.

Acknowledgments

A dance performance on stage ends with an agradecimento. Performers form a human line between the stage and the seats, hold hands, and bow together in gratitude. We do this, in relative silence, with our bodies. At the conclusion of this book, I am seated at a desk, seeking language for my gratitude to everyone who had a hand in its making. Public art involves the labor of numerous people, places, natural and human-made resources. These essays are memories of co-creation in schools, homes, and communities. I am grateful to everyone who appears in this book and behind the scenes. I've been shaped by our time together, and I appreciate you.

Thanks to the good people at Unsolicited Press for their kindness, structure, and interest in creating a second book with me. Thank you, Summer, for including me in your year of highlighting women authors. Thank you, Gayle Brandeis, for your example, generosity, and for helping me conjure a new life. Thank you Deena Metzger for modeling a writer's life and for keeping me close. Writing ethnography is a learned skill. I am very grateful to my research mentors Anastasia Loukaitou-Sideris, Marta Savigliano, Leobardo Estrada, and to Jeff Tobin.

I am grateful to the lovely humans at Community of Writers, Brenda Hillman, Imagining America, Jan Cohen-Cruz, PBS SoCal, Juan Devis, Carren Jao, Angela Boisvert, Denise Grande, Deborah Barndt, Margarita Antonio, Checo Valdez, Vera Caldas, the ArtsBridge Scholars, faculty, teachers, and students I had the pleasure of working with at UCLA and Claremont Graduate University,

La'Tonya Rease Miles, Marina Magalhães, T.J. Dedeaux-Norris, Tim Rice, Kori Hamilton, Thomas Turner, Leah Bass Bayliss, Aurea Montes-Rodriguez, the Community Coalition, the Children's Defense Fund, the LA Cultural Affairs Department, Janice Ngan, Brittany Campbell, Manuela C. Garcia, Las Colibri, Jazmin Morales, Dan Bellm, Lisa Pozas, The Autry Museum, Metro Arts, Betty Avila, Ben Caldwell, Francis Cullado, Jilly Canizares, Alma Catalán, Brittany Fields, Joel Garcia, Miranda Ynez, Self Help Graphics & Art, Kaos Network, Visual Communications, Georgia Harrell, Daniela Stigh, The Jewish Museum, Rabbi Yonasan Perry, Ana Rita Santiago, Tatiana Pequeno, UNEB, Nosakhare Collins, Libretto Magazine, my parents, siblings, and cousins. All the little and big homies who have conspired with me over the years.

I give thanks to the journals and outlets that published earlier versions of essays that appear in this book:: "Arts Education for the Next Generation of Culture Makers," *PBS SoCal*, 2020; "Born in Los Angeles on Los Angeles Street," Besos y Versos, *ASAP/J*, 2020, "Creative Justice: Arts Education for the City," *Public*, Journal of Imagining America, 2017; "Do Our Lives Matter?" Education, Citizenship, and Social Justice, *Sage Publications,* 2018, "Conectando los Puntos," HURACAN, *Viva! Arte Comunitaria y la Educacion Popular,* "Connecting the Dots" *SUNY Press* in *Viva: Community Art and Popular Education in the Americas;* "How to Become Erasure Proof," Geo Humanities, *GeoHumanities: Space, Place, and the Humanities,* Fall 2021; "My Grandma Was a Radical," *Tiferet Journal,* 2017; "Facing East" was first published in an earlier form as "Objects Tell Stories: Rosenbaum's Mizrah Over Six Generations," *The Jewish Museum,* 2023. I am also grateful to Writers' Project Ghana and Libretto Magazine where I developed ideas that informed "Pep Talk for Culture Makers."

I close with gratitude for my two great blessings: Avila and Reva. It's been an honor to witness them learn to decipher themselves, each other, and their mother. At tough moments they've found humor in our improvised meals, and always laughed and danced to celebrate our many breakthroughs. They never gawked at my desire for a life of continuous learning, and they have schooled me in the possibility of unconditional love. They continue to inspire me and elevate our lives beyond measure.

Notes

"Creative Justice"

1. Faith Davis and Exploring the Arts supported the EM project.

2. More information on Safe Routes to School is available through the National Center for Safe Routes to School at http://www.saferoutesinfo.org/.

3. The project process book is available open source at https://elaramobility.files.wordpress.com/2015/05/elaramoves_ebook 1.pdf.

4. Orlando Fals Borda said, "We act with our hearts but we also apply the brain. When we combine these two things, we are *sentipensantes* [feeling-thinking people]" (Fals Borda 2015). The notion of *Sentipensante* influenced Eduardo Galeano's literary philosophy and became critical to community arts praxis in Latin America. See *¡Viva! Community Arts and Popular Education in the Americas* (Barndt 2011).

5. While Los Angeles is known for car culture, freeways, congestion, and air contamination, the region continues to take strides to transform its transit infrastructure and air quality.

6. Richard Florida described the creative economy as a "tectonic force . . . upending our jobs, lives, and communities" (2005, vii). Maria Rosario Jackson (2014) noted that communities of color strengthen cities and regions by providing a sense of identity, place, and social cohesion.

7. Freire wrote, "A book reflects its author's confrontation with the world" (1985, 3).

8. Purifoy was a master sculptor and installation artist. He also led the Watts Towers Art Center and served on the California Arts Council Board shaping arts policy.

9. At the time this essay was written, census data found that 31% of East Los Angeles residents were 18 or under and 92% were Latine. 88% spoke a language other than English at home; and 43% were foreign born.

10. Erasure poems are created by erasing words from an existing piece of prose or poetry to create new meaning. This method is a form of found poetry.

11. Bike-share systems provide bike access to rent or borrow a bicycle from a bike dispensary and return it to another location in a service area.

"Do Our Lives Matter?"

1. Pseudonyms are used for the students' first names in this essay.

2. In the November 2016 election, Angelenos repealed a ban on bilingual education, approved more lenient parole rules for non-violent felons, passed a bond measure to help curb homelessness, and instituted a number of gun controls.

3. Latine is a gender-neutral term inclusive of Latino, Latina, and gender non-conforming diasporic Latin American identities.

"Connecting the Dots"

1. For more information, see Lawrence B. Graaf, Kevin Mulroy, Quintard Taylor, Seeking El Dorado: African Americans in California (Seattle: University of Washington Press, 2001).

2. Los Angeles is a landscape of ethnic and economic enclaves. In Los Angeles, one will find a vital "Chinatown," "Thai Town," "Historic FilipinoTown," "Korea Town," "Little India," "Little Armenia," "Little Ethiopia," and many more. These ethno-geographical designations suggest alternative cultural maps and are a strategy that has been used for communities to claim space and make Los Angeles feel more like home.

3. See Richard Valencia, The Mexican American Struggle for Equal Educational Opportunity in Mendez v. Westminster: Helping to Pave the Way for Brown v. Board of Education (Malden, MA: Blackwell, 2005).

4. The University of California is a public university that is a part of a multi-tiered system of public higher education in California that includes a network of community colleges and California State Universities.

5. Thomas Turner, Los Angeles, correspondence with author, 23 April, 2007.

6. For more information, see Amy Shimshon-Santo, "Arts Impact: Lessons from ArtsBridge," Journal for Teaching Through the Arts 6, 1 (2010), www.escholarship.org/uc/item/ 8je1p385#page-1, and read *Arts = Education* (UC Press, 2010).

7. Cynthia Wennstrom, Los Angeles, poetry assignment for ArtsBridge course, March 2, 2007.

8. Tameka Norris, written reflection for ArtsBridge course assignment, March 2008.

9. "Dropouts by Ethnic Designation by Grade," Los Angeles Unified School District for the Year 2007–2008, California Department of Edu- cation, Educational Demographics Office, prepared March 16, 2010.

10. Tameka Norris, written reflection, March 2008.

11. "Exercise My Rights," www.titleix.info, accessed March 16, 2010,

12. Norm Lacy, Santa Monica, correspondence with author, March 9, 2006.

13. Desiree Gallardo, Los Angeles, online blog, March 8, 2007.

14. Sonia Balonas, personal interview with author, Los Angeles, July 14, 2006.

15. A quinceañera is a traditional rite of passage ceremony that recognizes the transition from girlhood into womanhood. Its name in Spanish is drawn from the age at which it is usually performed, when a person is quince or fifteen years old.

16. Kris Gutierrez and Marjorie Orellana, "At Last: What's the Problem? Constructing Different Genres for the Study of English Learners," Research in the Teaching of English (RTE) 41.1 (2006):19.

17. Oscar Neal, public testimony at ArtsBridge citywide public gathering, Los Angeles, March 17, 2006.

"My Grandma Was a Radical"

1. My father used to tell me that his mother fell into the Black Sea when she was a girl and developed a lifelong fear of swimming. However, her life path crossed many oceans.

2. You can listen to Joachim Prinz's speech: https://www.youtube.com/watch?v=X0bwQsZnv0Y

3. Pogroms are organized massacres of specific ethnic groups. Anti-Jewish pogroms were commonplace in Reva's lifetime in Russia and Eastern Europe.

4. I am keenly aware of the sacrifices made for us to be able to express personal opinions publicly. Standing up against fascist behavior and injustice is a value I defend.

5. As a girl, I was fascinated by our family genealogies and my father helped me interview his dad Sidney, born Shloime, around 1974. I hadn't grown up near him, so I asked grandpa about his childhood. "What was school like? He laughed uncomfortably, as if to say you have no idea. "Jews didn't go to school," he said. His mother had been able to flee before him, but he waited nine years for her to save enough money to pay for his trip through Hamburg to New York. I asked him about his boat ride to the United States. "You wanted to die," he said. "No really, grandpa" I prodded. He repeated, "You wanted to die."

6. This section plays with Alice's infamous adventures with a caterpillar.

7. Grandma gave my father a goyisha (or non-Jewish) middle name, Bruce, that he could use as a last name if times got rough. He was born in 1932, before the war, but after the pogroms. She knew that protecting our children was of serious importance.

8. Egun is a Yoruba term for the ancestors. It is a word we use in my family that, through migration and marriage, has antecedents from five different continents, including Africa.

9. After I found the first FBI report that mentioned grandma by name, I wrote a letter to the Central Intelligence Agency requesting access to her complete file. They sent me back a letter referring me to the FBI. I wrote to the FBI explaining the referral and requesting her file. They replied in writing stating that her file had just been destroyed.

10. Accessed on January 26, 2017.

11. This article written by Mark Hensch published by *The Hill* demonstrates how history can be twisted and misrepresented if we don't remain vigilant for accuracy.

12. Office Memorandum, United States Government, From SA W. James Wood to SAC, Los Angeles (100-1763), December 3, 1958.

13. Office Memorandum, United States Government, From SA W. James Wood to SAC, Los Angeles (100-1763), December 3, 1958.

14. Dubois gave this speech "Socialism and the American Negro" in Madison Wisconsin in 1960.

15. From "Witness Spar at Red Hearing," Los Angeles Times, September 5, 1958.

"Facing East"

1. Israel Dov Rosenbaum's Mizrah was exhibited alongside Kehinde Wiley's painting in the exhibition *Kehinde Wiley/The World Stage: Israel* on view at the Jewish Museum from March to July 2012. It was most recently included in *Scenes from the Collection*, the Jewish Museum's collection exhibition, from January to June 2018, also installed next to the Wiley painting. Because it is a light-sensitive work, the mizrah cannot be exhibited for prolonged periods but an image of it is on the object label for Wiley's painting which is currently on view.

Works Cited

Academy of American Poets. 2017. "Found Poem: Poetic Form." https://www.poets.org/poetsorg/text/found-poem-poetic-form.

Anzaldúa, Gloria. 1987. *Borderlands: La Frontera: The New Mestiza*. San Francisco: Aunt Lute Books.

Askins, Kye. 2011. "Contact Zones: Participation, Materiality, and the Messiness of Interaction." *Environment and Planning D: Society and Space* 29: 803–821.

Bainter Cunningham, Sarah. 2013. "The Mute Child in the Creative City." Unpublished paper presented at *Face-to-Face*, New York City: Arts Education Roundtable. Referenced with permission.

Barndt, Deborah, ed. 2011. *¡Viva! Community Arts and Popular Education in the Americas*. New York: SUNY Press.

Barone, Tom, and Eliot W. Eisner. 2012. *Arts-Based Research*. Los Angeles: Sage Publications.

Bautista, Elvia. 2006. "Remembering All the Boys." Accessed March 10, 2015. http://thisibelieve.org/essay/21255/.

Bell, Derrick. 2005. "Doing the State Some Service." In *Paul Robeson: Artist and Citizen*, edited by Stewart J., 49–58. New Brunswick, NJ: Rutgers University Press.

Blake, G. 1958. "Witnesses Spar at Red Hearing." *Los Angeles Times*, September 5.

Blueprint for Creative Schools. 2015. Sacramento: CREATE CA. http://www.cde.ca.gov/eo/in/documents/bfcsreport.pdf.

Borda, Orlando Fals. 2006. "The North–South Convergence: A 30-Year First-Person Assessment of PAR." *Action Research* 4 (3): 351–358.

———. 2013. "Action Research in the Convergence of Disciplines." Translated by L. M. Sander. *International Journal of Action Research* 9 (2): 155–167.

Broyles-González, Yolanda. 1994. *El Teatro Campesino: Theater in the Chicano Movement.* Austin, TX: University of Texas Press.

Carroll, Lewis. 1865. *Alice's Adventures in Wonderland and Through the Looking Glass*, New York: Bantam.

Carter, Shawn. 2003. *The Black Album.* NY: Roc-A-Fella Records.

Catterall, James. 2009. *Doing Well and Doing Good by Doing Art.* Los Angeles, CA: Imagination Group.

Catterall, James, Susan Dumais, and Gillian Hampden-Thompson. 2012. *The Arts and Achievement in At-Risk Youth: Findings from Four Longitudinal Studies.* Washington, DC: National Endowment for the Arts.

Césaire, Aimé. 2017. *The Complete Poetry of Aimé Césaire.* Middletown, CT: Wesleyan University Press.

Chen, Anna. 2015. "The Future of Urban Planning: Students from East Los Angeles Renaissance Academy Visit Metro." Los Angeles: Metro LA. Accessed September 1, 2015. http://thesource.metro.net/2015/04/29/the-future-of-urban-planning-students-from-east-los-angeles-renaissance-academy-visit-metro/.

Children's Defense Fund. 2018. "Mission." http://www.childrensdefense.org/.

Coates, Ta-Nehisi. 2015. "Hope and the Historians: Writers Who Commit Themselves to Only Writing Hopeful Things Are Committing Themselves to the Ahistorical and the Mythical." *The Atlantic,* December 10.

Community Coalition. 2016. "History." www.cocosouthla.org.

CREATE CA. 2016. *Blueprint for Creative Schools.* http://www.cde.ca.gov/eo/in/documents/bfcsreport.pdf.

Crenshaw, Kimberlé. 1991. "Mapping the Margins: Intersectionality, Identity Politics, and Violence Against Women of Color." *Stanford Law Review* 43 (6): 1241–1299.

Dabashi, Hamid. 2015. *Can Non-Europeans Think?* London: Zed Books.

Derrida, Jacques. 1994. "What Is Ideology?" In *Specters of Marx: The State of the Debt, the Work of Mourning, and the New International,* translated by Peggy Kamuf. New York: Routledge.

De Sousa Santos, Buenaventura. 2014. *Epistemologies of the South: Justice against Epistemicide.* London: Routledge.

Dimension Films (Producer) and Robert Rodriguez (Director). 2001. *Spy Kids* [Motion Picture]. United States: Miramax Films.

Do Nascimento, Abdias. 1992. *Africans in Brazil: A Pan-African Perspective.* Trenton, NJ: African World Press.

Du Bois, W. E. B. 1926. "The Criteria of Negro Art." *The Crisis* 32: 290–297.

Ellis, Carolyn. 2009. *Revision: Autoethnographic Reflections on Life and Work.* London: Routledge.

Fals Borda, Orlando. 2013. "Action Research in the Convergence of Disciplines." Translated by Luis Marcos Sanders. *International Journal of Action Research* 9 (2): 155–167.

———. 2015. *Orlando Fals Borda – Sentipensante.* Interview. Accessed November 5, 2015. https://www.youtube.com/watch?v=LbJWqetRuMo.

Fantin, Monica. 2011. "Beyond Babel: Multiliteracies in Digital Culture." *International Journal of Digital Literacy and Digital Competence* 2 (1): 1–6.

Florida, Richard. 2005. *Cities and the Creative Class.* New York: Routledge.

Freire, Paulo. 1970. *Pedagogy of the Oppressed.* New York: Bloomsbury.

———. 1985. *The Politics of Education: Culture, Power, and Liberation.* Westport, CT: Bergin & Garvey.

Gardner, Howard. *Frames of Mind: The Theory of Multiple Intelligences.* New York: Basic Books.

_____. 1993. *Multiple Intelligences: The Theory in Practice.* New York: Basic Books.

Ginwright, Shawn. 1983. *Hope and Healing in Urban Education.* London: Routledge.

Greenfader, Christa Mulker, Liane Brouillette, and George Farkas. 2015. "Effect of a Performing Arts Program on the Oral Language Skills of Young English Learners." *Reading Research Quarterly* 50 (2): 185–203. https://doi.org/10.1002/rrq.90.

Hanley, Mary Stone, and George W. Noblit. 2009. *Cultural Responsiveness, Racial Identity, and Academic Success: A Review of Literature.* Pittsburgh: The Heinz Endowments.

Hanley, Mary Stone, and George W. Noblit. 2009. *Cultural Responsiveness, Racial Identity, and Academic Success: A Review of Literature.* Pittsburgh: The Heinz Endowments.

Harding, Sandra, ed. 1987. *Feminism and Methodologies: Social Science Issues.* Bloomington: Indiana University Press.

Haslem, Tahara. 2016. "Ineligibility." CREO. https://soundcloud.com/user-243356882/ineligibility-a-poem-by-takara.

Hayes, Terrance. 2010. "Lighthead's Guide to Addiction." https://www.poets.org/poetsorg/poem/light-heads-guide-addiction-audio-only.

———. 2015. *How to Draw an Invisible Man.* London: Penguin Books.

Hearings Before the Committee on Un-American Activities. 1958. *Testimony of Reva Mucha Zwolinski, House of Representatives, 85th Congress, Second Session, Part 2.* Washington, D.C.: United States Government Printing Offices, September 4 and 5. https://archive.org/stream/HUACEBF4154/HUAC-EBF-4154_djvu.txt.

Hecht. 1958. "Red Hearing, 4 September 1958. Mrs. Reva Zwolinski (Witness)." Caption slip reads: "Photographer: Hecht. Date: 1958-09-04. Reporter: Kline. Assignment: Red Hearing. 39: Mrs. Reva Zwolinski (Witness)." *Los Angeles Examiner Negatives Collection, 1950–1961* (subcollection). University of Southern California. https://digitallibrary.usc.edu/asset-management/2A3BF1WYPCOM.

Hensch, M. 2016. "Gingrich: Revive the House Un-American Activities Committee." *The Hill.* http://thehill.com/blogs/ballot-box/283511-gingrich-revive-house-un-american-activities-committee.

Hill-Collins, Patricia. 2008. *Black Feminist Thought: Knowledge, Consciousness, and the Politics of Empowerment.* Abington: Routledge.

Jackson, Maria Rosario. 2014. "What Are the Makings of a Healthy Community?" In *The Role of Artists and the Arts in Creative Placemaking.* Washington, DC: Goethe Institute.

James, C. L. R. 1963. *Beyond a Boundary.* London: Stanley Paul.

Kamenetz, Anya. 2015. "Nonacademic Skills Are Key to Success. But What Should We Call Them?" Accessed May 28, 2015. http://www.npr.org/sections/ed/2015/05/28/404684712/non-academic-skills-are-key-to-success-but-what-should-we-call-them.

Klein, Jim, and Julia Reichart, Producers and Directors. 1983. *Seeing Red: Histories of American Communists.* United States.

Lewis, C. 1865. *Alice's Adventures in Wonderland and Through the Looking Glass.* New York: Bantam.

Lipsitz, George. 2006. *The Possessive Investment in Whiteness: How White People Profit from Identity Politics.* Philadelphia, PA: Temple University Press.

———. 2011. *How Racism Takes Place.* Philadelphia, PA: Temple University Press.

Lorde, Audre. 1984. *Sister Outsider: Essays and Speeches by Audre Lorde.* Berkeley, CA: Crossing Press.

Los Angeles County Arts Commission. 2017. *Strengthening Diversity, Equity, and Inclusion in the Arts and Culture Sector for All Los Angeles County Residents.* https://www.lacountyarts.org/ceii-report.

Los Angeles County Housing Authority (LAHSA). 2017. *Greater Los Angeles Homeless Count—Data Summary—Council District.* https://www.lahsa.org/documents?id=1363-2017-homeless-count-results-council-district-8.pdf.

Lucas, G. 2012. "Teaching Visual Literacy and Communications." https://www.youtube.com/watch?v=GwDXlA_6usI.

Maeda, John. 2014. "From Storytelling to Storylistening: John Maeda." *Future of Storytelling.* Accessed June 1, 2015. https://www.youtube.com/watch?v=U8-Q70gV2Yk.

Markusen, Ann, and Anne Gadwa. 2010. *Creative Placemaking.* Washington, DC: National Endowment for the Arts.

Martin, Randy. 1990. *Performance as Political Act: The Embodied Self.* New York: Bergin & Garvey Publishers.

Mason, William. *Los Angeles under the Spanish Flag: Spain's New World.* Burbank, CA: Southern California Genealogical Society. http://www.scgsgenealogy.com/free/media/los-angeles-under-the-spanish-flag-wmason.pdf (accessed April 2, 2018).

Masters, Nathan. 2012. "L.A.'s First Freeways." Los Angeles: KCET. Accessed July 14, 2015. http://www.kcet.org/updaily/socal_focus/history/la-as-subject/las-first-freeways.html.

McGahan, J. 2017. "25 Years after the Riots: What a Teenager Learning Walking Home through the Flames." *LA Weekly.* http://www.laweekly.com/news/25th-anniversary-of-the-la-riots-a-teenager-recalls-walking-through-a-city-in-flames-8119455.

McIntyre, Alice. 2000. *Inner City Kids: Adolescents Confront Life and Violence in an Urban Community.* New York: New York University Press.

McKittrick, Katherine, and Clyde Woods. 2007. *Black Geographies and the Politics of Place.* Cambridge, MA: South End Press.

Mihalik, L., A. Pesce, and B. Welsh. 2016. "California 2016 Election Results." http://graphics.latimes.com/la-na-pol-2016-election-results-california.

Morrison, Toni. 1990. *Playing in the Dark: Whiteness and the Literary Imagination.* New York: Vintage Books.

Move LA. 2015. "Transit Rich Places." Los Angeles. Accessed August 22, 2015. http://www.movela.org/transit_rich_places.

Moore, Carlos. 2009. *Fela: This Bitch of a Life.* Chicago, IL: Chicago Review Press.

Morrison, Toni. 1990. *Playing in the Dark: Whiteness and the Literary Imagination.* New York: Vintage Books.

National Center for Safe Routes to School. 2015. "Safe Routes." Accessed January 5, 2015. http://www.saferoutesinfo.org.

Ortner, Sherry. 1974. "Is Female to Male as Nature Is to Culture?" In *Woman, Culture, and Society,* edited by M. Z. Rosaldo and L. Lamphere, 68–87. Stanford, CA: Stanford University Press.

Prinz, Joachim. 1963. "Speaks at the March on Washington for Civil Rights." YouTube video. https://www.youtube.com/watch?v=X0bwQsZnv0Y.

Public Testimony. 2015a. *Class Rehearsal for Open Mic, Esteban Torres High School,* Los Angeles, CA, May 22, 2015.

———. 2015b. *Open Mic, Esteban Torres High School,* Los Angeles, CA, May 27, 2015.

Ransby, Barbara. 2003. *Ella Baker and the Black Freedom Movement: A Radical Democratic Vision*. Chapel Hill, NC: University of North Carolina Press.

"Reds Use Fair to Pass Propaganda: Communist Group Hoists Russ Flag at World Trade Show." 1952. *Los Angeles Times,* May 19.

"Reva Mucha: World Trade Week." n.d. *Los Angeles Examiner Collection, 1920–1961,* USC Libraries, Los Angeles. http://usclibstore.usc.edu/search/?n=uscdiglib&scope=node&scopeValue =mpQGn&c=photos&q=reva+mucha+zwolinski#q=reva+mucha

Robinson, Ken. 2001. *Out of Our Minds: Learning to Be Creative*. Chichester, UK: Capstone.

Rolling, James Haywood Jr. 2013a. *Swarm Intelligence: What Nature Teaches Us About Shaping Creative Intelligence*. New York: St. Martin's Press.

———. 2013b. *Arts-Based Research*. New York: Peter Lang Publishing.

Santo, Avila. 2017a. *COCO Field Recording Day: COCO Composition #1*. Los Angeles, CA: CREO. https://www.soundcloud.com/user-243356882/coco-field-recording-a-day-at-usc.

Santo, Reva. 2017b. *COCO Art Lab (Online)*. Los Angeles, CA: CREO. https://www.youtube.com/watch?v=cPX8xQ0mmd0.

Shihab-Nye, Naomi. 2009. "Poetry Everywhere: 'One Boy Told Me' by Naomi Shihab Nye." https://www.youtube.com/watch?v=biJ3FP8aDjY.

Shimshon-Santo, Amy, ed. 2010a. *Arts = Education: Connecting Learning Communities in Los Angeles.* Irvine, CA: Center for Learning Through the Arts and Technology, UC Irvine, distributed by UC Press. https://escholarship.org/uc/item/5zp4c70w

———. 2010b. "Arts Impact: Lessons from ArtsBridge." *Journal for Learning Through the Arts,* 6 (1).

———. 2015. *#Elara Moves.* Los Angeles: Creo.

———. 2010b. "Arts Impact: Lessons from ArtsBridge." *Journal for Learning through the Arts* 6 (1): 1–13. https://files.eric.ed.gov/fulltext/EJ1093574.pdf.

———. 2017. "Creative Justice: Arts Education for the City." *Public: A Journal of Imagining America* 4 (1).

———. 2018. "Understanding Creative Vitality Through Data." *Sotheby's Institute of Art.* https://www.sothebysinstitute.com/news-and-events/news/understanding-creative-vitality-through-data/.

ShivHans Pictures (Producer) and J. Roach (Director). 2015. *Trumbo* [Motion Picture]. United States: Bleecker Street.

Sirmans, Franklin, and Yael Lipschutz. 2015. *Noah Purifoy: Junk Dada.* New York: Prestel, in conjunction with the Los Angeles County Museum of Art.

State Education Agency Directors of Arts Education (SAEDAE). 2014. *National Arts Education Standards: Dance, Music, Media Art, Music, Theater and Visual Arts.* https://nationalartsstandards.org.

State Education Directors of Arts Education. 2016. *National Core Arts Standards: Dance, Media Arts, Music, Theater and Visual Arts.* http://www.nationalartsstandards.org/.

Tufekci, Zeynep, and D. Talbot. 2016. "Remaking Social Media for the Next Revolution." *MIT Technology Review* 119 (3): 26–27.

United Nations General Assembly. 1948. *The Universal Declaration of Human Rights* (enacted).

United States Census Bureau. 2015. "Quick Facts." http://quickfacts.census.gov/qfd/states/06/06037.html.

Walker, D. 2018. "Justice over Greatness." *Ford Foundation Blog.* https://www.fordfoundation.org/ideas/equals-change-blog/posts/justice-over-greatness-a-new-years-reflection/.

W.E.B. Du Bois Speaks! Socialism and the American Negro (Full). 1948. YouTube video. https://www.youtube.com/watch?v=kKXglS90qn4.

Weiss, Cynthia. 2008. *AIMprint: New Relationships in the Arts and Learning.* Chicago, IL: Columbia College Chicago.

Woods, Clyde. 1998. *Development Arrested: The Blues and Plantation Power in the Mississippi Delta.* New York: Verso Books.

Young, Iris Marion. 1997. *Intersecting Voices.* Princeton, NJ: Princeton University Press.

About the Author

Dr. Amy Shimshon-Santo is the author of *Random Experiments in Bioluminescence* (Flowersong Press, 2024), *Catastrophic Molting* (Flowersong Press, 2022), *Even the Milky Way is Undocumented* (Unsolicited Press, 2020), and the limited edition chapbook *Endless Bowls of Sky* (Placeholder Press, 2020). Her essays have appeared in numerous academic journals including *Geo Humanities; Urban Education; Education, Citizenship, and Social Justice;* and *Imagining America.* She has edited *Et Al.: New Voices in Arts Management* with Genevieve Kaplan (IOPN, 2020); *Arts = Education* (UC Press, 2010); *Corpos, gêneros e literatura de autoria feminina* with Ana Rita Santiago and Tatiana Pequeno (Revista de Crítica Cultura, 2023); *Songs of the Earth* with Yvette Cabrera (LAPL, 2024), and *Consciousness* for Libretto Publishers (Nigeria, 2024). She was on the founding team of CREATE CA and co-lead led the equity policy work group for California's *Blueprint for Creative Schools* with Dr. Mary Stone Hanley. Amy enjoyed a fulfilling career in dance before co-founding the Brasil Brasil Cultural Center and directing two academic programs: Artsbridge (UCLA Arts), and Arts Management (Claremont Graduate University). She has been nominated for an Emmy Award, Pushcart Prizes in poetry and creative nonfiction, a Rainbow Reads Award, Best of the Net in Poetry, and was a finalist for the Nightboat Book Poetry Prize. She has been recognized on the National Honor Roll for Service Learning. Amy earned a doctorate and M.A. in Urban Planning from UCLA, and M.F.A. in Creative Writing from Antioch University, and a B.A. in Latin American Studies from UC Santa Cruz.

About the Press

Unsolicited Press is based out of Portland, Oregon and focuses on the works of the unsung and underrepresented. As a womxn-owned, all-volunteer small publisher that doesn't worry about profits as much as championing exceptional literature, we have the privilege of partnering with authors skirting the fringes of the lit world. We've worked with emerging and award-winning authors such as Shann Ray, Amy Shimshon-Santo, Brook Bhagat, Kris Amos, Elisa Carlsen, Douglas Cole, and John W. Bateman.

Learn more at unsolicitedpress.com. Find us on X and instagram.

www.ingramcontent.com/pod-product-compliance
Lightning Source LLC
Chambersburg PA
CBHW020227130626
46549CB00005B/1780